The Jesse Tree

ERIC & SUZAN SAMMONS

The
Jesse
Tree

An Advent Devotion

Illustrations by
Madeline Stutzman

SOPHIA INSTITUTE PRESS
Manchester, New Hampshire

Cover Design: LUCAS Art & Design, Jenison, MI.
Cover image: WikiMedia Commons / Stumme_Tree_of_Jesse.jpg.

Sophia Institute Press
Box 5284, Manchester, NH 03108
1-800-888-9344

www.SophiaInstitute.com

Sophia Institute Press® is a registered trademark of Sophia Institute.

paperback ISBN 978-1-64413-724-6

ebook ISBN 978-1-64413-725-3

Library of Congress Control Number: 2022939611

First printing

This book is dedicated with love to

Kathy Bedel

who shared with us the Jesse Tree devotion

and promoted it to her children and students for many years.

CONTENTS

Introduction

The Gospel of Matthew begins with the well-known description of the genealogy of Jesus Christ. St. Matthew emphasized to his largely Jewish audience the real and deep connection of Jesus with the Hebrew people, showing that He was indeed the son of David. This connection became important not only for Jewish readers, but for all those who sought to understand whether Christ was truly the Messiah promised by the Hebrew prophets.

Through the centuries, the Church deepened her understanding of the people and events of the Old Testament. The Fathers of the Church came to see Abraham, Isaac, Jacob, and many others as having a special role as forerunners of Christ. These figures of the Hebrew Scriptures imaged Him in a dim way, preparing the world for His future coming. They played a vital part in the history of salvation and in God's unfolding revelation of Himself to mankind.

The Jesse Tree seeks to present visually that important family history of our Savior—a family history that in Christ becomes the history of our salvation.

The tradition of tracing Christ's genealogy in this way dates from medieval times—an eleventh-century illuminated manuscript contains a depiction of the Jesse Tree, and the twelfth-century Chartres Cathedral boasts a Jesse Tree stained glass window.

The name for this visual depiction of Christ's heritage arises from the passage in Isaiah that proclaims,

> There shall come forth a shoot from the stump [root] of Jesse,
> and a branch shall grow out of his roots.

And the Spirit of the Lord shall rest upon him,
  the spirit of wisdom and understanding,
  the spirit of counsel and might,
  the spirit of knowledge and the fear of the Lord.
And his delight shall be in the fear of the Lord. (Isa. 11:1–3)

Isaiah's contemporaries probably assumed that this "root of Jesse" was David, the great king of Israel. But the passage is also a foretelling of the coming of the Messiah, the descendant of David and future King of Kings.

During Advent the Church turns her attention to the coming of Jesus, making it the ideal season for the devotion we now call the Jesse Tree. Naturally enough, many families hang Jesse Tree ornaments on their Christmas trees. The Christmas tree originated, of course, in Germany, most likely with the (spiritual) mystery play presented on Christmas Eve in medieval times. This play's scenery included the Tree of Knowledge of Good and Evil, an evergreen tree hung with apples. The plot unfolded to show Eve picking the apple, and she and Adam both eating of it.

Even today many families hang apples on their Christmas trees to highlight the connection between the Original Sin and the birth of the Savior. "In order that we might live, it was needful that God should incarnate Himself and be put to death" (St. Gregory Nazianzus). In Eden a tree brought death through Adam's sin, but Christ's tree of death, the Cross, became a tree of life through His sacrifice (see Rom. 5:18).

As the days of Advent pass, the Jesse Tree helps us follow the course of salvation history from the creation of the first man and woman, to the great flood, to the patriarchs of the Jewish faith, to the prophets, to the immediate forerunners of Christ. As we trace God's plan for the salvation of the world, we see revealed in deeper and deeper ways the mystery of His great love for man.

May He bless you in this season as you make a pilgrimage through the family history of our Savior.

How to Use This Book

This book is designed to assist your Advent devotions by walking you and your family briefly through the history of our salvation in Christ. Truly, volumes could be—and have been—written on this topic, but the reflections here are for the purpose of daily prayer in the family.

In early November give some thought to your family's Jesse Tree logistics: Will you make your own ornaments or purchase them? Will you place them on the family's Christmas tree or will there be another, dedicated place for them—a small, separate tree; a banner depicting a tree; or a garland? What is the best time of day for your family to practice this devotion? Do you need to purchase or make anything for this project?

Having addressed these questions, you are ready for Advent and your family's Jesse Tree to begin for the year. You can expect the family reflections in this book to take from five to fifteen minutes each day. After the first Sunday in Advent, for which there is a blessing of the Jesse Tree, this book includes one symbol (ornament) for every day of Advent. For each symbol there is a corresponding Bible passage, followed by a reflection, then a prayer, and finally a "Dig Deeper" section.

After reading the Scripture passage, read aloud the reflection for that day, giving family members opportunities to ask and answer questions as you read.

Follow your Jesse Tree reflection each day with the prayer included for the day. On December 17-23, you will find that the closing prayer is the day's O Antiphon, another traditional devotion taken from the Vespers prayers of the last week of Advent.

If you wish, you can also read the "Dig Deeper" section, particularly if you have older children in the family. These additional reflections are intended to bring out another aspect of the day's symbol and Bible passage at a higher level than the main reflection.

Our hope is that the Dig Deeper sections along with the main reflections accommodate families with children in a wide age range. For younger children, pausing to ask questions as you read the Scripture passage or discuss the reflection will help ensure that they are following along.

As you know, every Advent season is not the same number of days! So, except for years when Christmas falls on a Sunday, you will not have the twenty-eight-day Advent that makes the one-ornament-a-day plan work perfectly. For shorter Advents, we recommend not skipping but doubling up on certain days during the second and/or third week of Advent.

When you double up, you can either read both Scripture passages, or briefly touch on the meaning of one of the symbols while reading and praying the full reflection for the other symbol. What works best for your family will depend on how much time you have and the ages and attention spans of your children. All the ornaments should still be added to your tree.

Since the first day of Advent can fall on any one of seven different dates each year (November 27 – December 3), there are seven possible variations for your Jesse Tree progression. The pages that follow provide a chart for each of these seven possibilities. To see which ornaments to double up on in a given year, first determine the date of the first Sunday of Advent, then refer to the appropriate chart. Note that when the first Sunday of Advent is November 27, you will not need to double up on any ornaments because Christmas will fall on a Sunday.

SUN.	MON.	TUES.	WED.	THU.	FRI.	SAT.
Nov. 27 Blessing of the tree	**Nov. 28** Creation *(World)*	**Nov. 29** Adam and Eve *(Apple)*	**Nov. 30** Noah *(Ark)*	**Dec. 1** Abraham *(Stars)*	**Dec. 2** Isaac *(Ram)*	**Dec. 3** Jacob *(Ladder)*
Dec. 4 Joseph *(Coat of Many Colors)*	**Dec. 5** Moses *(Tablets)*	**Dec. 6** Aaron *(Hand of Blessing)*	**Dec. 7** Samuel *(Lamp)*	**Dec. 8** David *(Harp)*	**Dec. 9** The Good Shepherd *(Staff)*	**Dec. 10** Solomon *(Crown)*
Dec. 11 Elijah *(Raven)*	**Dec. 12** Isaiah *(Tongs)*	**Dec. 13** Ezekiel *(Heart of Flesh)*	**Dec. 14** Nehemiah *(Church)*	**Dec. 15** Messiah *(Dawn)*	**Dec. 16** New Covenant *(River)*	**Dec. 17** Zechariah *(Censer)*
Dec. 18 Gabriel *(Angel)*	**Dec. 19** Mary *(Lilies)*	**Dec. 20** Mary *(Magnificat)*	**Dec. 21** John the Baptist *(Baptismal Font)*	**Dec. 22** Joseph *(Carpenter's Tools)*	**Dec. 23** The Wise Men *(Star of Bethlehem)*	**Dec. 24** Baby Jesus *(Manger)*

Sun.	Mon.	Tues.	Wed.	Thu.	Fri.	Sat.
Nov. 28	Nov. 29	Nov. 30	Dec. 1	Dec. 2	Dec. 3	Dec. 4
Blessing of the tree	Creation (World)	Adam and Eve (Apple)	Noah (Ark)	Abraham (Stars)	Isaac (Ram)	Jacob (Ladder)
Dec. 5	Dec. 6	Dec. 7	Dec. 8	Dec. 9	Dec. 10	Dec. 11
Joseph (Coat of Many Colors)	Moses (Tablets)	Aaron (Hand of Blessing)	Samuel (Lamp)	David (Harp)	The Good Shepherd (Staff)	Solomon (Crown)
Dec. 12	Dec. 13	Dec. 14	Dec. 15	Dec. 16	Dec. 17	Dec. 18
Elijah (Raven)	Isaiah (Tongs)	Ezekiel (Heart of Flesh)	Nehemiah (Church)	(Dawn & River)	Zechariah (Censer)	Gabriel (Angel)
Dec. 19	Dec. 20	Dec. 21	Dec. 22	Dec. 23	Dec. 24	
Mary (Lilies)	Mary (Magnificat)	John the Baptist (Baptismal Font)	Joseph (Carpenter's Tools)	The Wise Men (Star of Bethlehem)	Baby Jesus (Manger)	

Sun.	Mon.	Tues.	Wed.	Thu.	Fri.	Sat.
Nov. 29 Blessing of the tree	**Nov. 30** Creation *(World)*	**Dec. 1** Adam and Eve *(Apple)*	**Dec. 2** Noah *(Ark)*	**Dec. 3** Abraham *(Stars)*	**Dec. 4** Isaac *(Ram)*	**Dec. 5** Jacob *(Ladder)*
Dec. 6 Joseph *(Coat of Many Colors)*	**Dec. 7** Moses *(Tablets)*	**Dec. 8** Aaron *(Hand of Blessing)*	**Dec. 9** Samuel *(Lamp)*	**Dec. 10** David *(Harp)*	**Dec. 11** The Good Shepherd *(Staff)*	**Dec. 12** Solomon *(Crown)*
Dec. 13 Elijah *(Raven)*	**Dec. 14** Isaiah *(Tongs)*	**Dec. 15** *(Heart & Church)*	**Dec. 16** *(Dawn & River)*	**Dec. 17** Zechariah *(Censer)*	**Dec. 18** Gabriel *(Angel)*	**Dec. 19** Mary *(Lilies)*
Dec. 20 Mary *(Magnificat)*	**Dec. 21** John the Baptist *(Baptismal Font)*	**Dec. 22** Joseph *(Carpenter's Tools)*	**Dec. 23** The Wise Men *(Star of Bethlehem)*	**Dec. 24** Baby Jesus *(Manger)*		

SUN.	MON.	TUES.	WED.	THU.	FRI.	SAT.
Nov. 30 Blessing of the tree	**Dec. 1** Creation *(World)*	**Dec. 2** Adam and Eve *(Apple)*	**Dec. 3** Noah *(Ark)*	**Dec. 4** Abraham *(Stars)*	**Dec. 5** Isaac *(Ram)*	**Dec. 6** Jacob *(Ladder)*
Dec. 7 Joseph *(Coat of Many Colors)*	**Dec. 8** Moses *(Tablets)*	**Dec. 9** Aaron *(Hand of Blessing)*	**Dec. 10** Samuel *(Lamp)*	**Dec. 11** David *(Harp)*	**Dec. 12** The Good Shepherd *(Staff)*	**Dec. 13** Solomon *(Crown)*
Dec. 14 *(Raven & Tongs)*	**Dec. 15** *(Heart & Church)*	**Dec. 16** *(Dawn & River)*	**Dec. 17** Zechariah *(Censer)*	**Dec. 18** Gabriel *(Angel)*	**Dec. 19** Mary *(Lilies)*	**Dec. 20** Mary *(Magnificat)*
Dec. 21 John the Baptist *(Baptismal Font)*	**Dec. 22** Joseph *(Carpenter's Tools)*	**Dec. 23** The Wise Men *(Star of Bethlehem)*	**Dec. 24** Baby Jesus *(Manger)*			

SUN.	MON.	TUES.	WED.	THU.	FRI.	SAT.
Dec. 1 Blessing of the tree	**Dec. 2** Creation (World)	**Dec. 3** Adam and Eve (Apple)	**Dec. 4** Noah (Ark)	**Dec. 5** Abraham (Stars)	**Dec. 6** Isaac (Ram)	**Dec. 7** Jacob (Ladder)
Dec. 8 Joseph (Coat of Many Colors)	**Dec. 9** Moses (Tablets)	**Dec. 10** Aaron (Hand of Blessing)	**Dec. 11** Samuel (Lamp)	**Dec. 12** David (Harp)	**Dec. 13** (Staff & Crown)	**Dec. 14** (Raven & Tongs)
Dec. 15 (Heart & Church)	**Dec. 16** (Dawn & River)	**Dec. 17** Zechariah (Censer)	**Dec. 18** Gabriel (Angel)	**Dec. 19** Mary (Lilies)	**Dec. 20** Mary (Magnificat)	**Dec. 21** John the Baptist (Baptismal Font)
Dec. 22 Joseph (Carpenter's Tools)	**Dec. 23** The Wise Men (Star of Bethlehem)	**Dec. 24** Baby Jesus (Manger)				

Sun.	Mon.	Tues.	Wed.	Thu.	Fri.	Sat.
Dec. 2 Blessing of the tree	**Dec. 3** Creation (World)	**Dec. 4** Adam and Eve (Apple)	**Dec. 5** Noah (Ark)	**Dec. 6** Abraham (Stars)	**Dec. 7** Isaac (Ram)	**Dec. 8** Jacob (Ladder)
Dec. 9 Joseph (Coat of Many Colors)	**Dec. 10** Moses (Tablets)	**Dec. 11** Aaron (Hand of Blessing)	**Dec. 12** (Lamp & Harp)	**Dec. 13** (Staff & Crown)	**Dec. 14** (Raven & Tongs)	**Dec. 15** (Heart & Church)
Dec. 16 (Dawn & River)	**Dec. 17** Zechariah (Censer)	**Dec. 18** Gabriel (Angel)	**Dec. 19** Mary (Lilies)	**Dec. 20** Mary (Magnificat)	**Dec. 21** John the Baptist (Baptismal Font)	**Dec. 22** Joseph (Carpenter's Tools)
Dec. 23 The Wise Men (Star of Bethlehem)	**Dec. 24** Baby Jesus (Manger)					

Sun.	Mon.	Tues.	Wed.	Thu.	Fri.	Sat.
Dec. 3 Blessing of the tree	**Dec. 4** Creation *(World)*	**Dec. 5** Adam and Eve *(Apple)*	**Dec. 6** Noah *(Ark)*	**Dec. 7** Abraham *(Stars)*	**Dec. 8** Isaac *(Ram)*	**Dec. 9** Jacob *(Ladder)*
Dec. 10 Joseph *(Coat of Many Colors)*	**Dec. 11** *(Tablets & Hand of Blessing)*	**Dec. 12** *(Lamp & Harp)*	**Dec. 13** *(Staff & Crown)*	**Dec. 14** *(Raven & Tongs)*	**Dec. 15** *(Heart & Church)*	**Dec. 16** *(Dawn & River)*
Dec. 17 Zechariah *(Censer)*	**Dec. 18** Gabriel *(Angel)*	**Dec. 19** Mary *(Lilies)*	**Dec. 20** Mary *(Magnificat)*	**Dec. 21** John the Baptist *(Baptismal Font)*	**Dec. 22** Joseph *(Carpenter's Tools)*	**Dec. 23** The Wise Men *(Star of Bethlehem)*
Dec. 24 Baby Jesus *(Manger)*						

Jesse Tree
Devotions

Blessing of the Jesse Tree

Today is the first day of Advent. To prepare our family for the coming of the Lord at Christmas, we will begin our Jesse Tree. After today we will add an ornament to our Jesse Tree each day. The ornament will represent one important person or event in the history of the Old Covenant that led up to and prepared the world for the birth of Jesus.

We will begin today by asking for God's blessing on our Jesse Tree and on our Advent devotions. Our prayer comes from Psalm 96.

Father: Our help is in the name of the Lord:
All: Who made heaven and earth.

Antiphon (all): All the trees of the wood shout for joy before the Lord, for he comes.

Psalm 96

(This may be read by the father alone, or the family may divide into two groups and alternate the reading.)

O sing to the Lord a new song;
sing to the Lord, all the earth!
Sing to the Lord, bless his name;
tell of his salvation from day to day.

Declare his glory among the nations,
his marvelous works among all the peoples!
For great is the Lord, and greatly to be praised;
he is to be feared above all gods.

For all the gods of the peoples are idols;
but the Lord made the heavens.
Honor and majesty are before him;
strength and beauty are in his sanctuary.

Ascribe to the Lord, O families of the peoples,
ascribe to the Lord glory and strength!
Ascribe to the Lord the glory due his name;
bring an offering, and come into his courts!

Worship the Lord in holy array;
tremble before him, all the earth!
Say among the nations, "The Lord reigns!
Yea, the world is established, it shall never be moved;
he will judge the peoples with equity."

Let the heavens be glad, and let the earth rejoice;
let the sea roar, and all that fills it;
let the field exult, and everything in it!

Then shall all the trees of the wood sing for joy
before the Lord, for he comes,
for he comes to judge the earth.
He will judge the world with righteousness,
and the peoples with his truth.

Glory be to the Father and to the Son and to the Holy Spirit,
as it was in the beginning, is now, and ever shall be
world without end. Amen.

Antiphon (all): All the trees of the wood shout for joy before the Lord, for he comes.

Sprinkle the tree with holy water.

Creation

(World)

Genesis 1:1–5; 1:24–2:3

*In the beginning God created the heavens and the earth. The earth was
without form and void, and darkness was upon the face of the deep;
and the Spirit of God was moving over the face of the waters.*

*And God said, "Let there be light"; and there was light. And God
saw that the light was good; and God separated the light from the
darkness. God called the light Day, and the darkness he called Night.
And there was evening and there was morning, one day. . . .*

*And God said, "Let the earth bring forth living creatures according to their
kinds: cattle and creeping things and beasts of the earth according to their
kinds." And it was so. And God made the beasts of the earth according to
their kinds and the cattle according to their kinds, and everything that creeps
upon the ground according to its kind. And God saw that it was good.*

*Then God said, "Let us make man in our image, after our likeness; and let
them have dominion over the fish of the sea, and over the birds of the air, and
over the cattle, and over all the earth, and over every creeping thing that creeps
upon the earth." So God created man in his own image, in the image of God
he created him; male and female he created them. And God blessed them, and
God said to them, "Be fruitful and multiply, and fill the earth and subdue it;
and have dominion over the fish of the sea and over the birds of the air and over
every living thing that moves upon the earth." And God said, "Behold, I have
given you every plant yielding seed which is upon the face of all the earth, and
every tree with seed in its fruit; you shall have them for food. And to every beast
of the earth, and to every bird of the air, and to everything that creeps on the
earth, everything that has the breath of life, I have given every green plant for
food." And it was so. And God saw everything that he had made, and behold,
it was very good. And there was evening and there was morning, a sixth day.*

*Thus the heavens and the earth were finished, and all the host of
them. And on the seventh day God finished his work which he had
done, and he rested on the seventh day from all his work which he
had done. So God blessed the seventh day and hallowed it, because on
it God rested from all his work which he had done in creation.*

Reflection

Who made all things?

God is the Creator of Heaven and earth. We think of Him as the maker of the stars and the sky, the One who said, "Let there be light." But did He make your shoes? Did He make your cat? Did He make you?

When you create a painting, you use paper, a paintbrush, and paint. God, the author of life, made everything out of nothing. Your shoes wouldn't exist without Him ... neither would your cat ... neither would you!

There never has been and never will be anything created without Him. And, by His almighty power He keeps the whole world in existence. That means that without Him, nothing at all could be.

Why did God create everything?

God created the world so that we can know His love and goodness. He created man because He wanted to share with him His own infinite happiness. And all that He created, He calls "good."

Every story has a beginning, and the story of our salvation starts with the creation of the world. It starts—and it will end—with the infinite love of God.

Prayer

"Every good endowment and every perfect gift is from above, coming down from the Father of lights with whom there is no variation or shadow due to change" (James 1:17).

O Lord God,
Thank You for every good gift You have given our family.
Thank You for Your great love for us.
Give us the grace to respond to Your love.
We ask this through Jesus Christ our Lord. Amen.

Dig Deeper

God created us to know Him, to love Him, and to serve Him. In other words, we are made to respond to the great love He showed in creating us.

We can deepen our knowledge of God by reading the Sacred Scriptures each day. A daily reading of the Gospels, in particular, can help us know our Lord and His teachings.

Christ said the greatest commandment is to "love the Lord your God with all your heart, and with all your soul, and with all your mind" (Matt. 22:37). We are called to complete love. Every part of our lives should demonstrate our love for Him—how we worship, how we treat others, and how we live our lives.

The second great commandment is to "love your neighbor as yourself" (Matt. 22:39)—just as we are called to know God and to love Him, we are called to service. We serve God by serving others, especially the poor and needy among us.

Adam and Eve

(Apple)

Genesis 3:1–19

Now the serpent was more subtle than any other wild creature that the Lord God had made. He said to the woman, "Did God say, 'You shall not eat of any tree of the garden'?" And the woman said to the serpent, "We may eat of the fruit of the trees of the garden; but God said, 'You shall not eat of the fruit of the tree which is in the midst of the garden, neither shall you touch it, lest you die.'" But the serpent said to the woman, "You will not die. For God knows that when you eat of it your eyes will be opened, and you will be like God, knowing good and evil." So when the woman saw that the tree was good for food, and that it was a delight to the eyes, and that the tree was to be desired to make one wise, she took of its fruit and ate; and she also gave some to her husband, and he ate. Then the eyes of both were opened, and they knew that they were naked; and they sewed fig leaves together and made themselves aprons.

And they heard the sound of the Lord God walking in the garden in the cool of the day, and the man and his wife hid themselves from the presence of the Lord God among the trees of the garden. But the Lord God called to the man, and said to him, "Where are you?" And he said, "I heard the sound of thee in the garden, and I was afraid, because I was naked; and I hid myself." He said, "Who told you that you were naked? Have you eaten of the tree of which I commanded you not to eat?" The man said, "The woman whom thou gavest to be with me, she gave me fruit of the tree, and I ate." Then the Lord God said to the woman, "What is this that you have done?" The woman said, "The serpent beguiled me, and I ate." The Lord God said to the serpent,

"Because you have done this,
cursed are you above all cattle,
and above all wild animals;
upon your belly you shall go,
and dust you shall eat
all the days of your life.
I will put enmity between you and the woman,
and between your seed and her seed;

he shall bruise your head,
and you shall bruise his heel."

To the woman he said,

"I will greatly multiply your pain in childbearing;
in pain you shall bring forth children,
yet your desire shall be for your husband,
and he shall rule over you."

And to Adam he said,

"Because you have listened to the voice of your wife,
and have eaten of the tree
of which I commanded you,
'You shall not eat of it,'
cursed is the ground because of you;
in toil you shall eat of it all the days of your life;
thorns and thistles it shall bring forth to you;
and you shall eat the plants of the field.
In the sweat of your face
you shall eat bread
till you return to the ground,
for out of it you were taken;
you are dust,
and to dust you shall return."

Reflection

Adam and Eve were the first parents of all human beings. What did God command Adam and Eve regarding the trees of the Garden of Eden?

God told Adam and Eve not to eat of the fruit of the tree that grew in the middle of the garden. This was the tree of the knowledge of good and evil. God told them this out of love for them.

When they disobeyed Him, Adam and Eve committed the Original Sin. The apple on our Jesse Tree represents this sin of our first parents. Because Adam and Eve chose to disobey, sin and death came into the world. And, there was nothing man could do to repair this damage. We were helpless.

What happened to Adam and Eve next? And what did God promise them?

Adam and Eve had to leave the Garden of Eden. They had lost the union with God they had enjoyed before their sin. They had damaged their union with one another, too. But God promised them a Savior who would one day defeat sin and death: our Lord Jesus Christ.

Jesus is called the "New Adam." Through the tree in the garden, Adam brought sin and death into the world. But Christ's death on the tree of the Cross brings us new life. He restores man's broken friendship with God.

Eve was created without sin and became the mother of the human race. Who is the "New Eve"?

Prayer

Deliver me, O God,
from all my sins and from every evil.
Make me ever hold fast to Your commandments
and never allow me to be separated from you.
We ask this through Jesus Christ our Lord. Amen.

Dig Deeper

After the Fall, God said to Adam and Eve, "I will put enmity between you and the woman, and between your seed and her seed; he shall bruise your head, and you shall bruise his heel" (Gen. 3:15). This was the first promise of a Savior who would eventually defeat Satan and reconcile us to God.

It was also the promise of a woman who would have complete enmity with Satan: the Immaculate Virgin Mary. In the Immaculate Conception, the Mother of Jesus was conceived free from Original Sin. She became man's solitary boast: one to whom we can look as a model of the perfect human person.

Even in the midst of the tragedy of the Fall, God's mercy still shone forth in the promise of the coming Messiah and His Immaculate Mother.

Noah

(Ark)

Genesis 7:1–12; 8:15–17

Then the Lord said to Noah, "Go into the ark, you and all your household, for I have seen that you are righteous before me in this generation. Take with you seven pairs of all clean animals, the male and his mate; and a pair of the animals that are not clean, the male and his mate; and seven pairs of the birds of the air also, male and female, to keep their kind alive upon the face of all the earth. For in seven days I will send rain upon the earth forty days and forty nights; and every living thing that I have made I will blot out from the face of the ground." And Noah did all that the Lord had commanded him.

Noah was six hundred years old when the flood of waters came upon the earth. And Noah and his sons and his wife and his sons' wives with him went into the ark, to escape the waters of the flood. Of clean animals, and of animals that are not clean, and of birds, and of everything that creeps on the ground, two and two, male and female, went into the ark with Noah, as God had commanded Noah. And after seven days the waters of the flood came upon the earth.

In the six hundredth year of Noah's life, in the second month, on the seventeenth day of the month, on that day all the fountains of the great deep burst forth, and the windows of the heavens were opened. And rain fell upon the earth forty days and forty nights.

… Then God said to Noah, "Go forth from the ark, you and your wife, and your sons and your sons' wives with you. Bring forth with you every living thing that is with you of all flesh—birds and animals and every creeping thing that creeps on the earth—that they may breed abundantly on the earth, and be fruitful and multiply upon the earth."

Reflection

God showed His great mercy to Adam and Eve when He promised that a Savior would one day come. But after many years, the people of the earth had become evil.

God was unhappy with the wickedness of the human race. Yet He found one good man: Noah. So even though mankind deserved punishment, God's mercy acted through this one good man. Through Noah, God renewed His covenant promise with mankind. What is the sign of God's covenant with Noah?

The flood cleansed the earth of wickedness, but God also ensured that the beauty of His creation would survive the flood. The people and animals on the ark would reestablish life on earth after the flood was over. God blessed the family of Noah so that man could again prosper on the earth.

The ark sheltered the family of Noah and brought them safely through the dangers of the flood. God even made sure Noah had food enough for all the people and animals on board. In a similar way, the Church protects and nourishes us during our life on earth. This is possible because of the graces won for us by Christ.

Scripture calls Noah the last "righteous man" of his time. A righteous person is one who keeps the moral laws of God. He lives in a way that is pleasing to God. Noah is a symbol of our Lord Jesus. Christ was "righteous" in a way no created man could be. He brought the righteousness of Heaven down to earth in order to lift us up to God.

Prayer

O God,
look with mercy on those who do not believe in You.
Draw them to the fullness of faith in You in the Catholic Church.
We ask this through Jesus Christ our Lord. Amen.

Dig Deeper

Scripture tells us, "God's patience waited in the days of Noah, during the building of the ark, in which a few, that is, eight persons, were saved through water. Baptism, which corresponds to this, now saves you, not as a removal of dirt from the body but as an appeal to God for a clear conscience, through the resurrection of Jesus Christ" (1 Pet. 3:20–21).

The flood and the saving of Noah and his family through the ark is a "type" of Baptism. A type is a person or event from the past that foreshadows a future person or event. In this case, Noah's family was saved through the waters of the flood, which foreshadowed our salvation through the cleansing waters of Baptism.

Without Baptism, we are like the men and women of Noah's time who scoffed at him: burdened by our sins and destined to perish. In Baptism, however, we are given the graces necessary to live a holy life and be united with Christ.

Abraham

(Stars)

Genesis 12:1–7; 15:1–6

Now the Lord said to Abram, "Go from your country and your kindred and
your father's house to the land that I will show you. And I will make of you
a great nation, and I will bless you, and make your name great, so that you
will be a blessing. I will bless those who bless you, and him who curses you I
will curse; and by you all the families of the earth shall bless themselves."

So Abram went, as the Lord had told him; and Lot went with him. Abram
was seventy-five years old when he departed from Haran. And Abram took
Sar'ai his wife, and Lot his brother's son, and all their possessions which
they had gathered, and the persons that they had gotten in Haran; and they
set forth to go to the land of Canaan. When they had come to the land of
Canaan, Abram passed through the land to the place at Shechem, to the
oak of Moreh. At that time the Canaanites were in the land. Then the Lord
appeared to Abram, and said, "To your descendants I will give this land."
So he built there an altar to the Lord, who had appeared to him. . . .

After these things the word of the Lord came to Abram in a vision, "Fear
not, Abram, I am your shield; your reward shall be very great." But Abram
said, "O Lord God, what wilt thou give me, for I continue childless, and
the heir of my house is Elie'zer of Damascus?" And Abram said, "Behold,
thou hast given me no offspring; and a slave born in my house will be my
heir." And behold, the word of the Lord came to him, "This man shall not
be your heir; your own son shall be your heir." And he brought him outside
and said, "Look toward heaven, and number the stars, if you are able
to number them." Then he said to him, "So shall your descendants be."
And he believed the Lord; and he reckoned it to him as righteousness.

Reflection

Many hundreds of years after Abraham lived, his story is told again by the author of the Letter to the Hebrews in the New Testament. God called Abraham to leave his home behind and go to a new place. Abraham obeyed, "not knowing where he was to go" (Heb. 11:8). He made his home as best he could as a stranger in a foreign land. Abraham wasn't troubled by his move, because he was looking forward to what God had promised him. He believed God's word to him.

Abraham was so old that the author of Hebrews calls him "as good as dead" (Heb. 8:12)! Yet, though his wife Sarah was also old, the son God promised Abraham was born. Then, in time, came grandchildren ... and great-grandchildren ... and great-great-grandchildren ... and on and on—"as many as the stars of heaven."

Who is the greatest of all the descendants of Abraham?

From the new Hebrew nation God established through Abraham came God's own Son, Jesus Christ.

How has God's promise that Abraham's descendants would number like the stars in the sky come true?

It is through Jesus Christ that this promise came true. People of every nation and race have become His followers—more people than we could ever count. Followers of Jesus are His brothers and sisters. Through Baptism we are adopted into the family of Jesus, which is the family of Abraham.

Prayer

O God,
Your love for us is ever faithful.
May we always trust in Your mercy
and have hope for our salvation through Your Son.
We ask this through Jesus Christ our Lord. Amen.

Dig Deeper

St. Paul tells us that "it is men of faith who are the sons of Abraham" (Gal. 3:7). Faith was the great virtue of Abraham: he believed God even when what he was told seemed impossible. When we act in faith, we become heirs of Abraham.

Christians have debated the role of faith in salvation for centuries. Some say that "faith alone" saves us, but St. Paul made clear it is "faith working through love" that brings us salvation (Gal. 5:6). In other words, like Abraham, we must act on our faith, for "faith by itself, if it has no works, is dead" (James 2:17).

As we live to imitate the faith of Abraham, we must move beyond empty words or sentiments and instead put our faith into loving action. Then we become children of Abraham, our father in faith.

Isaac

(Ram)

Genesis 22:1–18

After these things God tested Abraham, and said to him, "Abraham!" And he said, "Here am I." He said, "Take your son, your only son Isaac, whom you love, and go to the land of Mori'ah, and offer him there as a burnt offering upon one of the mountains of which I shall tell you." So Abraham rose early in the morning, saddled his ass, and took two of his young men with him, and his son Isaac; and he cut the wood for the burnt offering, and arose and went to the place of which God had told him. On the third day Abraham lifted up his eyes and saw the place afar off. Then Abraham said to his young men, "Stay here with the ass; I and the lad will go yonder and worship, and come again to you." And Abraham took the wood of the burnt offering, and laid it on Isaac his son; and he took in his hand the fire and the knife. So they went both of them together. And Isaac said to his father Abraham, "My father!" And he said, "Here am I, my son." He said, "Behold, the fire and the wood; but where is the lamb for a burnt offering?" Abraham said, "God will provide himself the lamb for a burnt offering, my son." So they went both of them together.

When they came to the place of which God had told him, Abraham built an altar there, and laid the wood in order, and bound Isaac his son, and laid him on the altar, upon the wood. Then Abraham put forth his hand, and took the knife to slay his son. But the angel of the Lord called to him from heaven, and said, "Abraham, Abraham!" And he said, "Here am I." He said, "Do not lay your hand on the lad or do anything to him; for now I know that you fear God, seeing you have not withheld your son, your only son, from me." And Abraham lifted up his eyes and looked, and behold, behind him was a ram, caught in a thicket by his horns; and Abraham went and took the ram, and offered it up as a burnt offering instead of his son. So Abraham called the name of that place The Lord will provide; as it is said to this day, "On the mount of the Lord it shall be provided."

And the angel of the Lord called to Abraham a second time from heaven, and said, "By myself I have sworn, says the Lord, because you have done this, and have not withheld your son, your only son, I will indeed bless

*you, and I will multiply your descendants as the stars of heaven and as
the sand which is on the seashore. And your descendants shall possess
the gate of their enemies, and by your descendants shall all the nations
of the earth bless themselves, because you have obeyed my voice."*

Reflection

What did God ask Abraham to do?

He asked Abraham to do the unthinkable: to sacrifice his son, Isaac. Abraham responded with great trust and faith in God. He was willing to obey God in all things, even if it meant giving up Isaac.

On their way up the mountain, Isaac asked his father where the animal was for the sacrifice. Abraham told him that God Himself would provide the lamb.

Abraham, when he answered Isaac this way, did not yet know that he would not have to sacrifice his son. He said what he did because he knew that God Himself had provided Isaac to him. Isaac did not belong to him, Abraham knew, but to God.

Abraham's words came to have greater meaning than he realized when he answered Isaac's question. First, "God Himself" did "provide the lamb." The angel stopped Abraham from harming his son, and Abraham discovered a ram in the bushes to sacrifice instead.

Though God spared Abraham's son, He did not spare His own. Thousands of years later, God would again "provide a lamb": His only begotten Son, Jesus Christ, whose sacrifice would save mankind.

St. John the Baptist called our Lord something that reminds us of the sacrifice of Isaac. What was it?

Prayer

O my God,
I firmly believe that You are one God in three divine persons,
Father, Son and Holy Spirit.

I believe that Your divine Son became man and died for our sins,
and that He will come to judge the living and the dead.
I believe these and all the truths which the holy Catholic Church teaches,
because You have revealed them,
who can neither deceive nor be deceived. Amen. *(Act of Faith)*

Dig Deeper

The Letter to the Hebrews gives a great testament to the faith of Abraham:

> By faith Abraham, when he was tested, offered up Isaac, and he who had received the promises was ready to offer up his only son, of whom it was said, "Through Isaac shall your descendants be named." He considered that God was able to raise men even from the dead; hence he did receive him back, and this was a symbol. (Heb. 11:17–19)

The offering of Isaac not only foreshadows the sacrifice of Jesus Christ on the Cross, but it also points to the Resurrection. For, Abraham was willing to do whatever God asked, even sacrificing his beloved son, because he knew that God could do anything—including raise someone from the dead.

This is a faith shared by the Blessed Virgin Mary on Calvary. She wept and was sorrowful over the death of her Son, but she knew that this mysterious event was part of God's plan. It was not the end of the story. She knew that the end of those who follow her Son was a resurrected glorious life for all eternity.

Jacob

(Ladder)

Genesis 28:10–17

Jacob left Beer-sheba, and went toward Haran. And he came to a certain place, and stayed there that night, because the sun had set. Taking one of the stones of the place, he put it under his head and lay down in that place to sleep. And he dreamed that there was a ladder set up on the earth, and the top of it reached to heaven; and behold, the angels of God were ascending and descending on it! And behold, the Lord stood above it and said, "I am the Lord, the God of Abraham your father and the God of Isaac; the land on which you lie I will give to you and to your descendants; and your descendants shall be like the dust of the earth, and you shall spread abroad to the west and to the east and to the north and to the south; and by you and your descendants shall all the families of the earth bless themselves. Behold, I am with you and will keep you wherever you go, and will bring you back to this land; for I will not leave you until I have done that of which I have spoken to you." Then Jacob awoke from his sleep and said, "Surely the Lord is in this place; and I did not know it." And he was afraid, and said, "How awesome is this place! This is none other than the house of God, and this is the gate of heaven."

Reflection

Jacob dreamed of a ladder that reached between Heaven and earth. Who did he see going up and down the ladder?

God spoke to Jacob through this dream. Just as He promised Abraham, God told Jacob that his descendants would be countless. He promised that they would fill the earth.

When he woke up, Jacob said "Surely the Lord is in this place; and I did not know it." How easy it is to forget the work God is doing, how much we need His help, and all His promises to us.

Why does God act? Why does He work in the world? God's purpose is always to bring us to salvation—life with Him forever in Heaven. Sometimes Heaven seems so far away, so difficult to understand or reach. But just as God repeatedly called the Hebrew people like Abraham, Isaac, and Jacob to Himself, He is always calling us to Himself.

The ladder and the angels Jacob saw show that we cannot reach Him on our own. We need His help to reach Him.

That is why Christ came to earth: to be the one "ladder" that lets us reach Heaven. Because of Him and with the help of His grace we have the hope of Heaven.

While He was on earth, He set up the sacraments of the Church. That way, we can receive His grace. Our Lord said, "I am the way, and the truth, and the life; no one comes to the Father, but by me" (John 14:6).

Prayer

O my God,
relying on Your almighty power and infinite mercy and promises,
I hope to obtain pardon of my sins,
the help of Your grace,
and life everlasting,
through the merits of Jesus Christ,
my Lord and Redeemer. Amen. *(Act of Hope)*

Dig Deeper

Jesus is the "ladder" to Heaven and the sacraments are the steps of that ladder. It is through the sacraments that we unite ourselves to Christ and walk our path to Heaven.

St. Paul wrote, "Do you not know that all of us who have been baptized into Christ Jesus were baptized into his death? We were buried therefore with him by baptism into death, so that as Christ was raised from the dead by the glory of the Father, we too might walk in newness of life" (Rom. 6:3–4).

We see in this how the sacraments, beginning with Baptism, unite us to Christ. It is this union which makes us more like Him, which in turn draws us closer to Heaven. In order to ascend the ladder put before us, let us live a sacramental life, particularly by regularly going to Confession and receiving our Lord in the Blessed Sacrament.

Joseph

(Coat of Many Colors)

Genesis 37:2–8, 12–14, 17–21, 23–24, 28–36

Joseph, being seventeen years old, was shepherding the flock with his brothers; he was a lad with the sons of Bilhah and Zilpah, his father's wives; and Joseph brought an ill report of them to their father. Now Israel loved Joseph more than any other of his children, because he was the son of his old age; and he made him a long robe with sleeves. But when his brothers saw that their father loved him more than all his brothers, they hated him, and could not speak peaceably to him.

Now Joseph had a dream, and when he told it to his brothers they only hated him the more. He said to them, "Hear this dream which I have dreamed: behold, we were binding sheaves in the field, and lo, my sheaf arose and stood upright; and behold, your sheaves gathered round it, and bowed down to my sheaf." His brothers said to him, "Are you indeed to reign over us? Or are you indeed to have dominion over us?" So they hated him yet more for his dreams and for his words. . . .

Now his brothers went to pasture their father's flock near Shechem. And Israel said to Joseph, "Are not your brothers pasturing the flock at Shechem? Come, I will send you to them." And he said to him, "Here I am." So he said to him, "Go now, see if it is well with your brothers, and with the flock; and bring me word again." So he sent him from the valley of Hebron, and he came to Shechem. . . . So Joseph went after his brothers, and found them at Dothan. They saw him afar off, and before he came near to them they conspired against him to kill him. They said to one another, "Here comes this dreamer. Come now, let us kill him and throw him into one of the pits; then we shall say that a wild beast has devoured him, and we shall see what will become of his dreams." But when Reuben heard it, he delivered him out of their hands, saying, "Let us not take his life." . . . So when Joseph came to his brothers, they stripped him of his robe, the long robe with sleeves that he wore; and they took him and cast him into a pit. The pit was empty, there was no water in it. . . .

Then Mid'ianite traders passed by; and they drew Joseph up and lifted him out of the pit, and sold him to the Ish'maelites for twenty shekels of silver; and they took Joseph to Egypt.

When Reuben returned to the pit and saw that Joseph was not in the pit, he rent his clothes and returned to his brothers, and said, "The lad is gone; and I, where shall I go?" Then they took Joseph's robe, and killed a goat, and dipped the robe in the blood; and they sent the long robe with sleeves and brought it to their father, and said, "This we have found; see now whether it is your son's robe or not." And he recognized it, and said, "It is my son's robe; a wild beast has devoured him; Joseph is without doubt torn to pieces." Then Jacob rent his garments, and put sackcloth upon his loins, and mourned for his son many days. All his sons and all his daughters rose up to comfort him; but he refused to be comforted, and said, "No, I shall go down to Sheol to my son, mourning." Thus his father wept for him. Meanwhile the Mid'ianites had sold him in Egypt to Pot'i-phar, an officer of Pharaoh, the captain of the guard.

Reflection

Joseph's brothers envied him. They knew his father had a special place in his heart for their younger brother. They hated to hear Joseph talk about his dreams, because his dreams seemed to predict that Joseph would somehow be raised above them. In time, their anger toward Joseph led them to a terrible sin. What did they do?

They sold Joseph as a slave and lied to their father about it, making him believe Joseph had been killed. Joseph suffered greatly through the sins of his brothers. His father did, too.

Just as Joseph's brothers rejected him, our Lord was also rejected by His people. We see this even when He was a baby. The inns all refused Him—there was no room. King Herod then tried to kill Him. Later, when Christ preached about God's Kingdom, most people refused to listen. Eventually, this rejection led to our Lord's death, just as Joseph's brothers at first wanted to kill him.

God eventually used Joseph's terrible fate to save His people. Because Joseph was in Egypt and remained faithful to God, God used him to protect the Chosen People from a famine. They would have died without Joseph's help.

Likewise, the rejection of our Lord led to an amazing rescue. Through His death on the Cross, we are saved from the death of sin. In a time of famine people do not have what they need to live. Before Jesus came, people's souls were in a time of famine. Our Lord's death on the Cross was like Joseph opening the stores of grain to the people. Christ opens the gates of Heaven for us.

Prayer

"We know that in everything God works for good with those who love him, who are called according to his purpose." (Rom. 8:28)

Dig Deeper

Joseph is a type of Jesus, but he is also a type of our Lord's foster-father, St. Joseph.

- The patriarch Joseph was the son of Jacob (Gen. 35:24); St. Joseph was the son of Jacob (Matt. 1:16).

- The patriarch Joseph had dreams that revealed his future (Gen. 37:5); St. Joseph had dreams that revealed his future (Matt. 1:20; 2:13).

- The patriarch Joseph was forced to go to Egypt (Gen. 37:28); St. Joseph was forced to flee to Egypt to escape Herod (Matt. 2:13).

St. Joseph, like the patriarch Joseph, cared deeply for his family. He was charged with protecting and providing for the Son of God and the Blessed Virgin Mary. In doing so, he became a model for all husbands and fathers by putting his family before his own desires.

Moses

(Tablets)

Exodus 20:1–17

And God spoke all these words, saying,

*"I am the Lord your God, who brought you out of the
land of Egypt, out of the house of bondage.*

"You shall have no other gods before me.

*"You shall not make for yourself a graven image, or any likeness of anything
that is in heaven above, or that is in the earth beneath, or that is in the water
under the earth; you shall not bow down to them or serve them; for I the Lord
your God am a jealous God, visiting the iniquity of the fathers upon the children
to the third and the fourth generation of those who hate me, but showing
steadfast love to thousands of those who love me and keep my commandments.*

*"You shall not take the name of the Lord your God in vain; for the
Lord will not hold him guiltless who takes his name in vain.*

*"Remember the sabbath day, to keep it holy. Six days you shall labor, and do all
your work; but the seventh day is a sabbath to the Lord your God; in it you shall
not do any work, you, or your son, or your daughter, your manservant, or your
maidservant, or your cattle, or the sojourner who is within your gates; for in six
days the Lord made heaven and earth, the sea, and all that is in them, and rested
the seventh day; therefore the Lord blessed the sabbath day and hallowed it.*

*"Honor your father and your mother, that your days may be
long in the land which the Lord your God gives you.*

"You shall not kill.

"You shall not commit adultery.

"You shall not steal.

"You shall not bear false witness against your neighbor.

*"You shall not covet your neighbor's house; you shall not covet
your neighbor's wife, or his manservant, or his maidservant, or
his ox, or his ass, or anything that is your neighbor's."*

Reflection

What's the best way to understand how to take care of something like a car or a dishwasher? Just look at the directions—the owner's manual. It was written by the item's creator, so it will tell you all you need to know. The Ten Commandments are a little bit like an owner's manual for mankind. Following the directions God has given us means we are living as He created us to live.

"I am the Lord your God, who brought you out of the land of Egypt." This was what God said before He gave the Ten Commandments to Moses. He reminded Moses and the people of what He had done for them. He reminded them of His great love for them.

This helped the Hebrew people understand why they had to keep the commandments: for love of God. Yet they often failed. The Original Sin of Adam and Eve still made itself felt. It was easier to do wrong than to choose what was right.

Since Christ came into the world, our "proof" of God's love for us has been multiplied. Now, mankind has seen God. His love has been made visible: to see it, look at a crucifix.

Also, because Christ came to earth, man has something he didn't have before. Our Lord opened up a treasure chest for us: a treasury of grace. Grace, God's life in our souls, helps us do right. It helps us keep the commandments.

Prayer

"By the other virtues, we offer God what we possess; but by obedience, we offer ourselves to Him." (St. Gregory the Great)

O God,
strengthen us in the virtue of obedience,
and let it lead us to greater love of You.
We ask this through Jesus Christ our Lord. Amen.

Dig Deeper

By the time of Jesus, the Jews had hundreds and hundreds of commandments they were required to follow. Some of these came from God, but many others were man-made and actually kept people from God.

Because there were so many commandments, many religious thinkers of the time wanted to discover which was the greatest. One day a lawyer asked Jesus this question. Our Lord's answer was:

> *"You shall love the Lord your God with all your heart, and with all your soul, and with all your mind. This is the great and first commandment. And a second is like it, You shall love your neighbor as yourself" (Matt. 22:37–39).*

Christ was going to the heart of the matter: What is the purpose of the law? It is to help man love. Without love, following commandments will not draw us closer to God; in fact, obedience without love may build up our pride and ego. But when we put love above all, the commandments are no longer a burden. They become something we long to follow.

Aaron

(Hand of Blessing)

Numbers 6:22–27

The Lord said to Moses, "Say to Aaron and his sons, Thus you
shall bless the people of Israel: you shall say to them,

The Lord bless you and keep you:
The Lord make his face to shine upon you, and be gracious to you:
The Lord lift up his countenance upon you, and give you peace.

"So shall they put my name upon the people of Israel, and I will bless them."

Reflection

The ancient world, like today's world, was home to many different religions. Most of them got a lot of things wrong. For instance, other than the Hebrews, all ancient believers worshiped false gods.

They also had practices that pointed in the right direction. All the world's ancient religions included some kind of sacrifice. Sometimes crops were offered up, sometimes animals. Both crops and animals are valuable. People need them in order to live.

When He established Aaron and his family as the priests of the Hebrews, God showed His people that there was something the ancient religions got right: sacrifice does have a vital role in true worship. God showed that this natural desire of people to offer sacrifice was good.

You can probably think of an example of an animal that was sacrificed by the Hebrew people in the Old Covenant. What is it?

Priests offered these sacrificial victims—priests like those established through the family of Aaron. In the New Covenant, there is also a sacrifice: the Mass. And there is also a priest and a victim.

Of course, we see the priest at Mass—there can be no Mass without him. But he is standing in for the one high priest, our Lord Jesus Christ.

In the Mass, is the victim a lamb?

Yes and no. In the Mass, Christ is the victim. He is offered under the appearance of bread and wine. This offering is the same sacrifice as the sacrifice of the Cross. And what did St. John the Baptist call our Lord when he said "Behold …"?

Prayer

O God,
almighty and merciful,
grant us through the Holy Sacrifice of the Mass
joy and peace,
a holier life,
time to do penance,
grace and consolation of the Holy Spirit,
and perseverance in good works.
We ask this through Jesus Christ our Lord. Amen.

Dig Deeper

Before the coming of Christ, many sacrifices made up the Old Law. While all these sacrifices helped God's Chosen People draw closer to Him, none of them fully reconciled God with man.

The Mass is the sacrifice of the New Law. Mass is said every day around the world—does this mean that many sacrifices are still necessary?

No; the Mass is the re-presentation of the one sacrifice of Christ on Calvary. It is the means by which we are united across time and space to the Cross. While Christ's sacrifice was sufficient for the redemption of mankind, God gave us the Mass as a way to participate in that sacrifice, thus making the graces of redemption available to us.

Samuel

(Lamp)

1 Samuel 3:1–21

Now the boy Samuel was ministering to the Lord under Eli. And the
word of the Lord was rare in those days; there was no frequent vision.

At that time Eli, whose eyesight had begun to grow dim, so that he could not see,
was lying down in his own place; the lamp of God had not yet gone out, and
Samuel was lying down within the temple of the Lord, where the ark of God was.
Then the Lord called, "Samuel! Samuel!" and he said, "Here I am!" and ran
to Eli, and said, "Here I am, for you called me." But he said, "I did not call; lie
down again." So he went and lay down. And the Lord called again, "Samuel!"
and Samuel arose and went to Eli, and said, "Here I am, for you called me." But
he said, "I did not call, my son; lie down again." Now Samuel did not yet know
the Lord, and the word of the Lord had not yet been revealed to him. And the
Lord called Samuel again the third time. And he arose and went to Eli, and said,
"Here I am, for you called me." Then Eli perceived that the Lord was calling the
boy. Therefore Eli said to Samuel, "Go, lie down; and if he calls you, you shall say,
'Speak, Lord, for thy servant hears.'" So Samuel went and lay down in his place.

And the Lord came and stood forth, calling as at other times, "Samuel! Samuel!"
And Samuel said, "Speak, for thy servant hears." Then the Lord said to Samuel,
"Behold, I am about to do a thing in Israel, at which the two ears of every one
that hears it will tingle. On that day I will fulfil against Eli all that I have spoken
concerning his house, from beginning to end. And I tell him that I am about to
punish his house for ever, for the iniquity which he knew, because his sons were
blaspheming God, and he did not restrain them. Therefore I swear to the house of Eli
that the iniquity of Eli's house shall not be expiated by sacrifice or offering for ever."

Samuel lay until morning; then he opened the doors of the house of the
Lord. And Samuel was afraid to tell the vision to Eli. But Eli called
Samuel and said, "Samuel, my son." And he said, "Here I am." And
Eli said, "What was it that he told you? Do not hide it from me. May
God do so to you and more also, if you hide anything from me of all that
he told you." So Samuel told him everything and hid nothing from him.
And he said, "It is the Lord; let him do what seems good to him."

And Samuel grew, and the Lord was with him and let none of his words fall
to the ground. And all Israel from Dan to Beer-sheba knew that Samuel was
established as a prophet of the Lord. And the Lord appeared again at Shiloh,
for the Lord revealed himself to Samuel at Shiloh by the word of the Lord.

Reflection

The first verse of this reading tells us that "the word of the Lord was rare in those days." This is a sign that the Hebrew people at this time were not very close to God.

When God calls to Samuel, at first neither he nor Eli realize what is happening. God must repeat Himself three times. Sometimes people are slow to listen to the voice of the Lord.

God speaks, not usually with a roar, but more often in a "still small voice" (1 Kings 19:12). This "voice" may come to us as the voice of our pastor, who has a special responsibility to teach us God's commands. It may be the voice of our parents, our main teachers in the Faith. We also hear the voice of our conscience: the judgments we make in our hearts that tell us right from wrong.

Sometimes God calls people to a special mission. He told Samuel to preach the coming of a Messiah who would rule all people. God also calls people to their vocations, whether the priesthood, religious life, or marriage. Even now, God is preparing you to discover what your vocation is.

God speaks to us about everyday things, too. Through our consciences and the teachings of the Church, He helps us know right and wrong. He even helps us in choices between two right things, to know which is better—more wise or more loving.

What can we do to make ourselves ready to hear and understand what God wants of us?

Prayer

Teach us, Good Lord,
to serve You as You deserve;
to give and not to count the cost;
to fight and not to heed the wounds;
to labor and not to ask for any reward,
save that of knowing that we do Your will.
Through Jesus Christ our Lord. Amen. *(St. Ignatius of Loyola)*

Dig Deeper

Next time you see your pastor, ask him about his vocation story. How did he decide to become a priest? It's likely his story won't include anything too dramatic like a voice from Heaven or a vision in a dream. Most priestly vocation stories are about men hearing God through their parents, friends, and holy men and women.

The same is likely the case about how your parents met each other, fell in love, and got married. God didn't speak directly to bring your parents together, but instead spoke through a number of people and events to make your family.

Every person has a vocation, and it's important to pray fervently to know what your vocation is. If you are a young man, it might be the priesthood. If you are a young woman, it might be the religious life. Perhaps you are called to marriage. No matter what the call, listen to the voice of God, however it comes to you.

David

(Harp)

1 Samuel 16:1–13

The Lord said to Samuel, "How long will you grieve over Saul, seeing I
have rejected him from being king over Israel? Fill your horn with oil, and
go; I will send you to Jesse the Bethlehemite, for I have provided for myself
a king among his sons." And Samuel said, "How can I go? If Saul hears
it, he will kill me." And the Lord said, "Take a heifer with you, and say,
'I have come to sacrifice to the Lord.' And invite Jesse to the sacrifice,
and I will show you what you shall do; and you shall anoint for me him
whom I name to you." Samuel did what the Lord commanded, and came
to Bethlehem. The elders of the city came to meet him trembling, and said,
"Do you come peaceably?" And he said, "Peaceably; I have come to sacrifice
to the Lord; consecrate yourselves, and come with me to the sacrifice." And
he consecrated Jesse and his sons, and invited them to the sacrifice.

When they came, he looked on Eli'ab and thought, "Surely the Lord's anointed
is before him." But the Lord said to Samuel, "Do not look on his appearance
or on the height of his stature, because I have rejected him; for the Lord
sees not as man sees; man looks on the outward appearance, but the Lord
looks on the heart." Then Jesse called Abin'adab, and made him pass before
Samuel. And he said, "Neither has the Lord chosen this one." Then Jesse made
Shammah pass by. And he said, "Neither has the Lord chosen this one." And
Jesse made seven of his sons pass before Samuel. And Samuel said to Jesse,
"The Lord has not chosen these." And Samuel said to Jesse, "Are all your sons
here?" And he said, "There remains yet the youngest, but behold, he is keeping
the sheep." And Samuel said to Jesse, "Send and fetch him; for we will not
sit down till he comes here." And he sent, and brought him in. Now he was
ruddy, and had beautiful eyes, and was handsome. And the Lord said, "Arise,
anoint him; for this is he." Then Samuel took the horn of oil, and anointed
him in the midst of his brothers; and the Spirit of the Lord came mightily upon
David from that day forward. And Samuel rose up, and went to Ramah.

Reflection

God asked Samuel to anoint a new king. How did Samuel know which son of Jesse to pick? Wouldn't it make sense to choose the oldest son? Or perhaps the one who seemed strongest or wisest? Samuel didn't choose the oldest or strongest or wisest. As each brother came before him, he simply waited for God to show him the one He wanted.

God chose young David. God did not look at David's appearance, He looked at his heart. There He saw love, courage, and devotion. He saw a young man who would serve Him with his whole being. David would become the most celebrated figure in the Old Testament, a "man after [God's] own heart" (Acts 13:22), but to human eyes he seemed small and insignificant.

Jesus also seemed an unlikely king: born in a stable, hardly educated (see John 7:15), with nowhere, even, "to lay his head" (Luke 9:58). And what kind of king has a cross for a throne, a crown made of thorns, and, for a court, dozens of taunting soldiers and religious leaders?

God's ways are not our ways. Often we must look more deeply into things to see His work. He may act in ways that don't make sense to us.

That is when we must turn back to the things we do know. We know that God loves us. We know that He wants us to be happy with Him in Heaven. We know that He cares for us, knows all things, and can do all things. Remembering these truths will help us through times that are hard or confusing.

Prayer

O God,
form me as a child after Your own heart.
Help me turn away from sin
and become more and more who You made me to be.
We ask this through Jesus Christ our Lord. Amen.

Dig Deeper

In the history of salvation, God chose certain men for important roles: Noah, Abraham, Moses, and David are a few examples. Another man chosen for a special role was St. Peter, the leader of the apostles and the first pope.

Like David, St. Peter at first seemed inadequate to the task given to him. He was a lowly fisherman, impulsive and given to quick judgment. This was the man that would lead the Church?

The first returns were not promising: right after being given the keys to the Kingdom of Heaven, Peter was called "Satan" by Jesus for urging Him to forsake His path of suffering (see Matt. 16:23). Then Peter publicly denied Jesus three times and abandoned Him to the Cross.

Yet this is the man chosen by God, and eventually he converted thousands and gave his life for his Lord. Our Lord chooses each of us for a purpose—although not usually a purpose as grandiose as David's or Peter's. No matter our natural talents, if we are faithful to His call, we will be able to carry out His plan for us.

The Good Shepherd

(Staff)

Psalm 23

The Lord is my shepherd, I shall not want;
he makes me lie down in green pastures.
He leads me beside still waters;
he restores my soul.
He leads me in paths of righteousness
for his name's sake.

Even though I walk through the valley of the shadow of death,
I fear no evil;
for thou art with me;
thy rod and thy staff,
they comfort me.

Thou preparest a table before me
in the presence of my enemies;
thou anointest my head with oil,
my cup overflows.
Surely goodness and mercy shall follow me
all the days of my life;
and I shall dwell in the house of the Lord
for ever.

Reflection

The Scriptures often mention shepherds, the guardians of that simple animal, the sheep. David, who wrote the psalms, was a shepherd himself. Then God called him to lead the nation of Israel, and he became a shepherd of God's people.

What does a shepherd do?

Psalm 23 helps us first think of the shepherd as one who cares for both the bodily and spiritual needs of his sheep. Green pastures and still waters provide food and water for their physical needs, as well as peace for the soul.

The shepherd leads his sheep "in the paths of righteousness." The righteous way is the way of living that pleases God. The shepherd does not just point this way out to the sheep; he leads them on it. He teaches them righteousness by example.

The way will not always be easy. There will be times of "darkness." There will be suffering and difficulty. Yet, we can know what awaits us. One day our Good Shepherd will give us all that we need in abundance: "my cup overflows."

Jesus, our Good Shepherd, our Example and Guide, lays down His life for His sheep.

Prayer

O God,
give us new strength from the courage of Christ,
our Savior and Redeemer.
He is our Good Shepherd;
let us hear the sound of His voice;
lead our steps in the path He has shown,
that we may receive His help
and one day enjoy the light of your presence forever in Heaven.
We ask this through Jesus Christ our Lord. Amen.

Dig Deeper

When we think of sheep, it's likely that what comes to mind is their docility. Sheep are easily led. If we are to be sheep in Christ's flock, then we must be docile to His will.

Docility, however, does not come naturally to most of us. We want to do our will, not someone else's will, even if it's Christ's. We think if we do what we want, then we'll be happy and fulfilled. Our modern world pushes this message relentlessly: fulfillment comes from doing things "my way."

Yet true joy and peace comes not from doing our will, but by doing God's will. He knows far better than we do what makes us whole and complete. Whenever we resist this will, we find only pain and misery. By modeling ourselves on sheep, we discover pastures more beautiful than we can imagine.

Solomon

(Crown)

1 Kings 3:3–15

Solomon loved the Lord, walking in the statutes of David his father; only, he sacrificed and burnt incense at the high places. And the king went to Gibeon to sacrifice there, for that was the great high place; Solomon used to offer a thousand burnt offerings upon that altar. At Gibeon the Lord appeared to Solomon in a dream by night; and God said, "Ask what I shall give you." And Solomon said, "Thou hast shown great and steadfast love to thy servant David my father, because he walked before thee in faithfulness, in righteousness, and in uprightness of heart toward thee; and thou hast kept for him this great and steadfast love, and hast given him a son to sit on his throne this day. And now, O Lord my God, thou hast made thy servant king in place of David my father, although I am but a little child; I do not know how to go out or come in. And thy servant is in the midst of thy people whom thou hast chosen, a great people, that cannot be numbered or counted for multitude. Give thy servant therefore an understanding mind to govern thy people, that I may discern between good and evil; for who is able to govern this thy great people?"

It pleased the Lord that Solomon had asked this. And God said to him, "Because you have asked this, and have not asked for yourself long life or riches or the life of your enemies, but have asked for yourself understanding to discern what is right, behold, I now do according to your word. Behold, I give you a wise and discerning mind, so that none like you has been before you and none like you shall arise after you. I give you also what you have not asked, both riches and honor, so that no other king shall compare with you, all your days. And if you will walk in my ways, keeping my statutes and my commandments, as your father David walked, then I will lengthen your days."

And Solomon awoke, and behold, it was a dream. Then he came to Jerusalem, and stood before the ark of the covenant of the Lord, and offered up burnt offerings and peace offerings, and made a feast for all his servants.

Reflection

Solomon loved the Lord. This is the first thing we read today. Next, we learn that he lived in a way pleasing to God. That's what it means when the verse says he "walk[ed] in the statutes of David his father." Because of his love for God, he always tried to keep the commandments.

When we love someone, we want to be like that person. Solomon wanted to be like God—holy and good. So when God asked him what gift he wanted, Solomon asked for wisdom. He knew that wisdom would help him to be more holy. It would help him to be a good king for the Chosen People.

Wisdom is not the same as knowledge. We don't become wise by reading a lot of books and doing well in school. Wisdom means seeing things the way God sees them. We have many choices to make each day. Should we say our prayers? Help our family? Be a good example to our friends? When we have to make these choices, wisdom helps us know the best answer. It helps us know how best to live God's commands.

Even though wisdom isn't the same as knowledge, learning about God and His world can help us become more wise. If we want to become like our Lord, we must get to know Him. We do this by listening to our parents and pastors as they teach us about our Catholic Faith. Reading about our Lord in the Bible, especially the Gospels, helps us get to know Him, too.

God was pleased that Solomon asked for wisdom. He will be pleased, too, if you ask Him for this virtue. God is happy to bless us with things that make us more like Him.

Prayer

Come Holy Spirit,
fill the hearts of Your faithful and kindle in them the fire of Your love.
Send forth Your Spirit and they shall be created.
And You shall renew the face of the earth.
O, God, who by the light of the Holy Spirit,
did instruct the hearts of the faithful,
grant that by the same Holy Spirit
we may be truly wise and ever enjoy His consolations,
through Christ our Lord. Amen.

Dig Deeper

The Scriptures tell us that "The fear of the Lord is the beginning of wisdom" (Prov. 9:10). This might seem odd at first glance: Wouldn't discipline or intelligence or education seem better starting points for becoming wise?

No. Wisdom, as we read above, is not the same thing as knowledge. It is seeing things from God's perspective, and doing that requires us first to recognize the vast gulf between God and man.

God is literally *awesome*, inspiring awe for His greatness and majesty. This is what "fear of the Lord" is — not a servile fear, but a deep-down recognition of our smallness in the presence of God.

Recognizing the vast difference between us and God then leads to a change in perspective. Instead of seeing the things of this world from a natural perspective, we see them with supernatural eyes, knowing that God is above all. He is always in control, no matter what may happen. This change in perspective is itself wisdom.

Elijah

(Raven)

1 Kings 17:1–16

*Now Eli'jah the Tishbite, of Tishbe in Gilead, said to Ahab, "As the Lord
the God of Israel lives, before whom I stand, there shall be neither dew nor
rain these years, except by my word." And the word of the Lord came to
him, "Depart from here and turn eastward, and hide yourself by the brook
Cherith, that is east of the Jordan. You shall drink from the brook, and I
have commanded the ravens to feed you there." So he went and did according
to the word of the Lord; he went and dwelt by the brook Cherith that is east
of the Jordan. And the ravens brought him bread and meat in the morning,
and bread and meat in the evening; and he drank from the brook. And
after a while the brook dried up, because there was no rain in the land.*

*Then the word of the Lord came to him, "Arise, go to Zar'ephath, which belongs
to Sidon, and dwell there. Behold, I have commanded a widow there to feed you."
So he arose and went to Zar'ephath; and when he came to the gate of the city,
behold, a widow was there gathering sticks; and he called to her and said, "Bring
me a little water in a vessel, that I may drink." And as she was going to bring it,
he called to her and said, "Bring me a morsel of bread in your hand." And she
said, "As the Lord your God lives, I have nothing baked, only a handful of meal
in a jar, and a little oil in a cruse; and now, I am gathering a couple of sticks,
that I may go in and prepare it for myself and my son, that we may eat it, and
die." And Eli'jah said to her, "Fear not; go and do as you have said; but first
make me a little cake of it and bring it to me, and afterward make for yourself
and your son. For thus says the Lord the God of Israel, 'The jar of meal shall
not be spent, and the cruse of oil shall not fail, until the day that the Lord sends
rain upon the earth.'" And she went and did as Eli'jah said; and she, and he,
and her household ate for many days. The jar of meal was not spent, neither did
the cruse of oil fail, according to the word of the Lord which he spoke by Eli'jah.*

Reflection

Elijah prophesied that a great famine was coming. A terrible drought would cause the waters of all the streams of the land to dry up. Without water, crops and animals die.

God directed Elijah to go to another region and live near a stream. There, God commanded the ravens to bring him food. Once the stream became dry, God told Elijah to ask a widow in a nearby village for water and food. Did the widow have any food to spare?

No, she was down to her last bit of flour and oil. With this she planned to make a last meal for herself and her son. Elijah told her of God's promise: "For thus says the Lord the God of Israel, 'The jar of meal shall not be spent, and the … oil shall not fail, until the day that the Lord sends rain upon the earth.'"

This promise was meant not just for the widow. It is for you and me. God's goodness and providence will never run out. He proves this to us in a very real way: "the jar of meal" for making bread reminds us of the Eucharist, the food God gives our souls for our pilgrimage on earth. The oil is like the chrism oil used at our Baptism and Confirmation. The graces of these sacraments will never be "used up."

Elijah depended on God completely. He knew that man can never reach the end of God's goodness. Our Lord also depended totally on the loving Father. His life on earth shows us how to trust always in God, the source of all life.

Prayer

O Christ Jesus,
when all is darkness and we feel our weakness and helplessness,
give us the sense of Your presence, Your love, and Your strength.
Help us to have perfect trust in Your protecting love and strengthening
    power,
so that nothing may frighten or worry us,
for, living close to You,
we shall see Your hand, Your purpose, Your will through all things. Amen.
    (St. Ignatius of Loyola)

Dig Deeper

During Christ's forty-day temptation in the desert, Satan challenged Jesus to throw Himself down from the Temple, quoting the Scripture, "'He will give his angels charge of you,' and 'On their hands they will bear you up, lest you strike your foot against a stone'" (Matt. 4:6).

As is his way, Satan was abusing the words of Scripture, confusing dependence with presumption. Our Lord promised that God will always care for us, reminding us that we should not be anxious about our lives (see Matt. 6:25). But depending on God is not the same thing as presuming on His providence. Jesus rebuked Satan: "You shall not tempt the Lord your God" (Matt. 4:7).

As we grow in our dependence on God, let us not presume on His mercy. In following His will we give ourselves over to His providence. He will always care for us.

Isaiah

(Tongs)

Isaiah 6:1–8

In the year that King Uzzi'ah died I saw the Lord sitting upon a throne, high and lifted up; and his train filled the temple. Above him stood the seraphim; each had six wings: with two he covered his face, and with two he covered his feet, and with two he flew. And one called to another and said:

"Holy, holy, holy is the Lord of hosts;
the whole earth is full of his glory."

And the foundations of the thresholds shook at the voice of him who called, and the house was filled with smoke. And I said: "Woe is me! For I am lost; for I am a man of unclean lips, and I dwell in the midst of a people of unclean lips; for my eyes have seen the King, the Lord of hosts!"

Then flew one of the seraphim to me, having in his hand a burning coal which he had taken with tongs from the altar. And he touched my mouth, and said: "Behold, this has touched your lips; your guilt is taken away, and your sin forgiven." And I heard the voice of the Lord saying, "Whom shall I send, and who will go for us?" Then I said, "Here am I! Send me."

Reflection

Imagine you have the chance to meet a great king or queen, but you must take a long journey before you arrive at the palace. On the way, mud splatters your clothes, your face and hands get dirty, and rain drenches your hair. Would you be saddened to enter the royal palace looking like this?

The prophet Isaiah had a vision of the holiness of God. Isaiah was amazed, but also fearful. He realized the unworthiness and sinfulness of himself and all men compared to God's great holiness. Like a muddy visitor to a royal palace, Isaiah felt that he did not belong in the presence of the Almighty.

Immediately, one of the angels near the throne of the Lord used tongs to take a hot ember from a fire. He touched it against Isaiah's lips. His sins were forgiven. He could then go forth to preach the Word of God.

We too must have our sins forgiven in order to do the work of God. Because of Christ's birth, life, death, and Resurrection, that forgiveness is available to us.

Through Baptism we are cleansed of the stain of Original Sin. Through the Sacrament of Confession we are forgiven of the sins we ourselves have committed.

Cleansed through the graces of the sacraments, we become free to "serve him without fear, in holiness and righteousness before him all the days of our life" (Luke 1:74-75).

Prayer

O Lord God,
I love You above all things,
and I love my neighbor for Your sake
because You are the highest, infinite and perfect good,
worthy of all my love.
In this love I intend to live and die. Amen. *(Act of Love)*

Dig Deeper

The words of the Seraphim that Isaiah hears should be familiar to Catholics:

> *Holy, holy, holy is the Lord of hosts;*
> *the whole earth is full of his glory. (Isa. 6:3)*

They of course remind us of the *Sanctus* at every Mass:

> *Holy, Holy, Holy Lord God of hosts.*
> *Heaven and earth are full of your glory.*
> *Hosanna in the highest.*
> *Blessed is he who comes in the name of the Lord.*
> *Hosanna in the highest.*

The response of Isaiah to his vision should be a model for our attitude at Mass. Isaiah says,

> *Woe is me! For I am lost; for I am a man of unclean lips, and I dwell in the midst of a people of unclean lips; for my eyes have seen the King, the Lord of hosts! (Isa. 6:5)*

Isaiah recognizes that he is in a holy place and that he is unworthy for such a great honor. The same is true for us sinners at Mass: Our Lord Himself comes down from His heavenly throne and becomes truly present at each and every Mass. We are not worthy to be present at an event of such tremendous majesty, but we can say with the Roman centurion, "Lord, I am not worthy to have you come under my roof; but only say the word, and my servant will be healed" (Matt. 8:8).

Ezekiel

(Heart of Flesh)

Ezekiel 36:22–36

"Therefore say to the house of Israel, Thus says the Lord God: It is not for
your sake, O house of Israel, that I am about to act, but for the sake of
my holy name, which you have profaned among the nations to which you
came. And I will vindicate the holiness of my great name, which has been
profaned among the nations, and which you have profaned among them;
and the nations will know that I am the Lord, says the Lord God, when
through you I vindicate my holiness before their eyes. For I will take you
from the nations, and gather you from all the countries, and bring you
into your own land. I will sprinkle clean water upon you, and you shall
be clean from all your uncleannesses, and from all your idols I will cleanse
you. A new heart I will give you, and a new spirit I will put within you;
and I will take out of your flesh the heart of stone and give you a heart of
flesh. And I will put my spirit within you, and cause you to walk in my
statutes and be careful to observe my ordinances. You shall dwell in the
land which I gave to your fathers; and you shall be my people, and I will
be your God. And I will deliver you from all your uncleannesses; and I will
summon the grain and make it abundant and lay no famine upon you. I
will make the fruit of the tree and the increase of the field abundant, that
you may never again suffer the disgrace of famine among the nations. Then
you will remember your evil ways, and your deeds that were not good; and
you will loathe yourselves for your iniquities and your abominable deeds.
It is not for your sake that I will act, says the Lord God; let that be known
to you. Be ashamed and confounded for your ways, O house of Israel.

"Thus says the Lord God: On the day that I cleanse you from all your iniquities,
I will cause the cities to be inhabited, and the waste places shall be rebuilt. And
the land that was desolate shall be tilled, instead of being the desolation that
it was in the sight of all who passed by. And they will say, 'This land that was
desolate has become like the garden of Eden; and the waste and desolate and
ruined cities are now inhabited and fortified.' Then the nations that are left
round about you shall know that I, the Lord, have rebuilt the ruined places, and
replanted that which was desolate; I, the Lord, have spoken, and I will do it.

Reflection

Through Ezekiel, God said that the Hebrew people had done wrong. They "profaned among the nations" God's name. What does this mean?

The Israelites failed to live the covenant they had with God. They were not faithful to His commands. God reminded His people of His profound holiness, which they had forgotten in the midst of their sin.

Sometimes we speak of an unloving person as having "a heart of stone." Stone cannot "feel." God described the heart of His Chosen People as being one of stone. They were no longer moved by love of Him. They were "unfeeling."

God promised that He would send salvation. Then they would repent of their evil deeds. Their sorrow for their sins will spring from the new heart He will give them, "a heart of flesh." This heart is capable of feeling and movement; unlike stone it can respond to the great love of God.

It is the goodness of God's mercy—not fear of His punishments—that will show forth the evil of sin. Even in the face of man's sin, God desires his love and repentance, not his death.

Christ is the complete fulfillment of God's mercy. He came to earth as a helpless baby to become one of us. He grew up to die for us, even though we are sinners (see Rom. 5:8).

Prayer

Lord, God all-powerful,
the solemnity of our redemption is near.
May it bring us the helps that are useful for our present life
and obtain for us the rewards of eternal happiness.
We ask this through our Lord, Jesus Christ. Amen.
(Adapted from the Ember Wednesday Collect of Advent)

Dig Deeper

In this vision of Ezekiel, the Lord promises to "sprinkle clean water upon you," "put my spirit within you," "deliver you from all your uncleannesses," and "summon the grain and make it abundant." These promises were magnificently fulfilled in the sacraments of Baptism, Confirmation, Penance, and the Eucharist. Look again at those promises:

Clean water — Baptism
My spirit within you — Confirmation
Delivery from uncleanness — Penance
Abundance of grain — Eucharist

By living a sacramental life, we are given the "new hearts" God promised to Ezekiel. This points to the transformational nature of the sacraments: they truly and really change us. When we are baptized, we are transformed into children of God, no longer with hearts of stone, but hearts of flesh. These new hearts allow us to become more like Christ every day, until we can say with St. Paul, "It is no longer I who live, but Christ who lives in me" (Gal. 2:20).

Nehemiah

(Church)

Nehemiah 13:15–22

In those days I saw in Judah men treading wine presses on the sabbath,
and bringing in heaps of grain and loading them on asses; and also wine,
grapes, figs, and all kinds of burdens, which they brought into Jerusalem on
the sabbath day; and I warned them on the day when they sold food. Men
of Tyre also, who lived in the city, brought in fish and all kinds of wares and
sold them on the sabbath to the people of Judah, and in Jerusalem. Then I
remonstrated with the nobles of Judah and said to them, "What is this evil
thing which you are doing, profaning the sabbath day? Did not your fathers
act in this way, and did not our God bring all this evil on us and on this
city? Yet you bring more wrath upon Israel by profaning the sabbath."

When it began to be dark at the gates of Jerusalem before the sabbath, I
commanded that the doors should be shut and gave orders that they should not
be opened until after the sabbath. And I set some of my servants over the gates,
that no burden might be brought in on the sabbath day. Then the merchants and
sellers of all kinds of wares lodged outside Jerusalem once or twice. But I warned
them and said to them, "Why do you lodge before the wall? If you do so again
I will lay hands on you." From that time on they did not come on the sabbath.
And I commanded the Levites that they should purify themselves and come and
guard the gates, to keep the sabbath day holy. Remember this also in my favor,
O my God, and spare me according to the greatness of thy steadfast love.

Reflection

When Nehemiah returned from a visit with a foreign king, he found a lot of things wrong among the Chosen People. For one thing, they were doing all sorts of hard work on the Sabbath day. They were more concerned with buying and selling than with the commands of God.

Remember what God did on the seventh day of Creation?

God Himself rested on that day. And then, in the Ten Commandments, He told us that the Sabbath is to be set aside for worship and rest.

Nehemiah was shocked to find that the people had abandoned the Sabbath rest. He commanded them forcefully to change their habits. He reminded them that their fathers and grandfathers had also broken the Sabbath rest, and look what happened to them! They were made captives. Nehemiah promised that their actions would only "bring more wrath upon Israel."

The people were slow to listen to Nehemiah, but he didn't give up. He was so sure of how important it is to obey God, that he was willing to do anything to change the people's behavior.

In Old Covenant times, the Sabbath was what we call Saturday. Now we honor the Sabbath on the first day of the week, Sunday. Why did this change?

But how well do we keep God's command to honor the Sabbath? Is Sunday a day for sports and shopping, or for worship, prayer, rest, and works of mercy?

Prayer

O God,
who on the new Sabbath,
through Your Only Begotten Son,
have conquered death and thrown open to us the gate of everlasting life,
grant, we pray, that we who keep holy the day of the Lord's Resurrection
may one day rise up in the light of life. Amen. (*Adapted from the Collect of Easter*)

Dig Deeper

The most important event of each week is Sunday Mass. It's so important that the Church has made it obligatory to attend unless we are prevented by a serious reason such as illness. While the Sabbath is often seen primarily as a day of rest, it can more accurately be described as a day of worship.

This day points toward our eternal rest in Heaven. But what will we be doing in Heaven? According to the book of Revelation, Heaven will consist of the eternal worship of God. Rest is worship, and worship is rest.

Rest, in this sense, is not sleeping or being lazy—it is being completely at peace with God and with oneself. Since we were created for the worship of God, it is only through worship that we truly can be at rest.

Messiah

(Dawn)

Isaiah 9:2–7

The people who walked in darkness
have seen a great light;
those who dwelt in a land of deep darkness,
on them has light shined.
Thou hast multiplied the nation,
thou hast increased its joy;
they rejoice before thee
as with joy at the harvest,
as men rejoice when they divide the spoil.
For the yoke of his burden,
and the staff for his shoulder,
the rod of his oppressor,
thou hast broken as on the day of Mid'ian.
For every boot of the tramping warrior in battle tumult
and every garment rolled in blood
will be burned as fuel for the fire.
For to us a child is born,
to us a son is given;
and the government will be upon his shoulder,
and his name will be called
"Wonderful Counselor, Mighty God,
Everlasting Father, Prince of Peace."
Of the increase of his government and of peace
there will be no end,
upon the throne of David, and over his kingdom,
to establish it, and to uphold it
with justice and with righteousness
from this time forth and for evermore.
The zeal of the Lord of hosts will do this.

Reflection

Have you ever woken up before dawn? Even though the night is dark, eventually you see the sky become lighter in the east. You cannot yet see the sun, but you see its light beginning to break through. When we see these first signs of dawn, we know that the sun will rise soon.

Isaiah compared the waiting of the Chosen People to that waiting for the first light of dawn. God inspired Isaiah to tell the people that this dawn—the Messiah—would surely come. Just as surely as the sun rises each morning.

Isaiah talked about the freedom God's people will finally have when the Savior comes. Over the years, they had been captives. They had been slaves. But worse, they had been defeated by sin. They were not able to overcome it.

It is our Lord Jesus who frees them from this dark time of slavery to sin. Isaiah said, "a child is born, to us a son is given." He said that this son will rule God's people, but He will not be like many of the rulers they've had before. Those rulers did not always love the people. They did not always show them how to obey God and live in freedom. Even when the people did have a good ruler, eventually that man died or was defeated.

But the Savior to come, our Lord Jesus, would rule with wisdom, might, and peace. And His rule would free people to obey the commands of God. His light would conquer darkness forever.

Prayer

Prepare us, O God,
for the time "when the day shall dawn upon us from on high
to give light to those who sit in darkness and in the shadow of death,
to guide our feet into the way of peace" (Luke 1:78–79).
We ask this through Jesus Christ our Lord. Amen.

Dig Deeper

The Old Testament is a time of darkness. Man wars against man, committing sin after sin in his attempt to be like God. Reading the Old Testament can seem depressing, as we see man's inhumanity fully displayed.

Yet that is not the whole story of the Old Testament. We also see God continually intervening to lead His people to salvation. In the long dark night of the Old Testament, God directs them to the coming light — His Son and our Savior, Jesus Christ.

When we are in our own dark nights, let us look to the light of the Lord, trusting that He is the "light [that] shines in the darkness, and the darkness has not overcome it" (John 1:5).

New Covenant

(River)

Ezekiel 47:1–12

*Then he brought me back to the door of the temple; and behold, water was
issuing from below the threshold of the temple toward the east (for the temple
faced east); and the water was flowing down from below the south end of the
threshold of the temple, south of the altar. Then he brought me out by way
of the north gate, and led me round on the outside to the outer gate, that
faces toward the east; and the water was coming out on the south side.*

Going on eastward with a line in his hand, the man measured a thousand cubits,
and then led me through the water; and it was ankle-deep. Again he measured
a thousand, and led me through the water; and it was knee-deep. Again he
measured a thousand, and led me through the water; and it was up to the loins.
Again he measured a thousand, and it was a river that I could not pass through,
for the water had risen; it was deep enough to swim in, a river that could not
be passed through. And he said to me, "Son of man, have you seen this?"

Then he led me back along the bank of the river. As I went back, I saw upon
the bank of the river very many trees on the one side and on the other. And he
said to me, "This water flows toward the eastern region and goes down into
the Arabah; and when it enters the stagnant waters of the sea, the water will
become fresh. And wherever the river goes every living creature which swarms
will live, and there will be very many fish; for this water goes there, that the
waters of the sea may become fresh; so everything will live where the river goes.
Fishermen will stand beside the sea; from En-ge'di to En-eg'laim it will be a
place for the spreading of nets; its fish will be of very many kinds, like the fish
of the Great Sea. But its swamps and marshes will not become fresh; they are
to be left for salt. And on the banks, on both sides of the river, there will grow
all kinds of trees for food. Their leaves will not wither nor their fruit fail, but
they will bear fresh fruit every month, because the water for them flows from
the sanctuary. Their fruit will be for food, and their leaves for healing."

Reflection

In the prophet Ezekiel's vision, a vast river flowed from the Temple. The water from this river produced abundant fish, trees, and fruit.

"This water flows toward the eastern region and goes down into the Arabah; and when it enters the stagnant waters of the sea, the water will become fresh." The sea at the location this verse describes is the Dead Sea.

Ezekiel's vision is a prophecy. It does not prophesy that the Dead Sea will literally become a sea of fresh water teeming with life. It tells of something even more amazing.

The water from the Temple symbolizes the sacramental waters of Baptism flowing from the Church. This water will flood the souls of the faithful to wash away Original Sin.

Without grace, our souls die. They are like the Dead Sea itself, where nothing can live. The Dead Sea is deadened by salt, but our souls can be deadened by sin.

Under the Old Covenant, God's people had no way to restore life to souls dead through sin. But a new age is about to dawn. The Savior of mankind is coming. Through the accomplishment of His mission, the river of grace will be established, and this grace will be available to all men.

The trees and the water are described as everlastingly refreshing. The graces of God will never be exhausted.

Prayer

O God,
give ear to our prayers
and by the grace of Your coming enlighten the darkness of our souls.
We ask this through Christ our Lord. Amen. (*Adapted from the Collect of the Third Sunday of Advent*)

Dig Deeper

The abundant river that flows from the Temple points to the overflowing graces we receive from the sacraments. Like the trees planted on each side of the river, we are nourished by the sacraments, which give us the strength to follow Christ faithfully.

The imagery of the trees on the riverside should remind us of our inability to be fruitful under our own power. Without the sun and the water, the trees would wither and die. Likewise, we will wither and die, spiritually, without the Son and the sacraments.

Let us plant ourselves firmly in the sacraments, the only way to our salvation.

Zechariah

(Censer)

Luke 1:5–25

In the days of Herod, king of Judea, there was a priest named Zechari'ah, of
the division of Abi'jah; and he had a wife of the daughters of Aaron, and her
name was Elizabeth. And they were both righteous before God, walking in
all the commandments and ordinances of the Lord blameless. But they had
no child, because Elizabeth was barren, and both were advanced in years.

Now while he was serving as priest before God when his division was on
duty, according to the custom of the priesthood, it fell to him by lot to enter
the temple of the Lord and burn incense. And the whole multitude of the
people were praying outside at the hour of incense. And there appeared to him
an angel of the Lord standing on the right side of the altar of incense. And
Zechari'ah was troubled when he saw him, and fear fell upon him. But the
angel said to him, "Do not be afraid, Zechari'ah, for your prayer is heard, and
your wife Elizabeth will bear you a son, and you shall call his name John.

And you will have joy and gladness,
and many will rejoice at his birth;
for he will be great before the Lord,
and he shall drink no wine nor strong drink,
and he will be filled with the Holy Spirit,
even from his mother's womb.
And he will turn many of the sons of Israel to the Lord their God,
and he will go before him in the spirit and power of Eli'jah,
to turn the hearts of the fathers to the children,
and the disobedient to the wisdom of the just,
to make ready for the Lord a people prepared."

And Zechari'ah said to the angel, "How shall I know this? For I am an old
man, and my wife is advanced in years." And the angel answered him, "I am
Gabriel, who stand in the presence of God; and I was sent to speak to you,
and to bring you this good news. And behold, you will be silent and unable
to speak until the day that these things come to pass, because you did not
believe my words, which will be fulfilled in their time." And the people were

waiting for Zechari'ah, and they wondered at his delay in the temple. And when he came out, he could not speak to them, and they perceived that he had seen a vision in the temple; and he made signs to them and remained dumb. And when his time of service was ended, he went to his home.

After these days his wife Elizabeth conceived, and for five months she hid herself, saying, "Thus the Lord has done to me in the days when he looked on me, to take away my reproach among men."

Reflection

Gabriel appeared to Zechariah to share the news of a beautiful gift from God. Zechariah and Elizabeth will have a son, even though they are old. How did Zechariah respond?

Zechariah asked, "How shall I know this? For I am an old man, and my wife is advanced in years." This may not seem like a bad question to us. We know that normally a child cannot be born to an old woman. But Gabriel could hear more in Zechariah's "reasonable" words. He knew that Zechariah doubted God's power.

God did not punish Zechariah for his doubt by refusing him the promised son; He simply made him silent. For nine months Zechariah could consider his mistake. During this time he was shown God's power. His wife conceived and then bore a son, just as Gabriel had promised.

How do you think Zechariah spent those silent months? We can probably find out by looking at how they ended. First, after his son was born, family members were debating what to name him. Zechariah wrote these words, "His name is John." This showed his obedience to Gabriel's message.

Then, finally, he could speak again. And he spoke only of God's goodness and mercy toward the Chosen People. He spoke of the great plan the Lord had for John, who would prepare the way for Jesus. Zechariah's confusion and doubt, through silence, were transformed into deep faith, joy, and trust in God.

Prayer

O Wisdom,
You came forth from the mouth of the Most High,
and reaching from beginning to end,
You ordered all things mightily and sweetly.
Come, and teach us the way of prudence! Amen. *(O Antiphon for December 17)*

Dig Deeper

Luke tells us that Zechariah and his wife Elizabeth were "righteous before God, walking in all the commandments and ordinances of the Lord blameless." Zechariah was also a Temple priest—an exemplar of the Jewish faith, one who knew in the depths of his being the promises of God.

In spite of this, Zechariah did not believe Gabriel when the angel told him of his own role in salvation history. While he awaited the coming Messiah like all Jews, Zechariah didn't think he himself would be instrumental in preparing for it.

We too can doubt our own roles in the salvation. Sharing the Faith is something we leave to others, not believing that we can prepare someone for the coming of Christ into his heart. We become silent like Zechariah when the Lord asks us to speak on His behalf. Let us put to work the Advent graces we receive to bring many others to the Christ Child.

Gabriel

(Angel)

Luke 1:26–38

In the sixth month the angel Gabriel was sent from God to a city of
Galilee named Nazareth, to a virgin betrothed to a man whose name was
Joseph, of the house of David; and the virgin's name was Mary. And he
came to her and said, "Hail, full of grace, the Lord is with you!" But she
was greatly troubled at the saying, and considered in her mind what sort
of greeting this might be. And the angel said to her, "Do not be afraid,
Mary, for you have found favor with God. And behold, you will conceive
in your womb and bear a son, and you shall call his name Jesus.

He will be great, and will be called the Son of the Most High;
and the Lord God will give to him the throne of his father David,
and he will reign over the house of Jacob for ever;
and of his kingdom there will be no end."

And Mary said to the angel, "How can this be, since I
have no husband?" And the angel said to her,

"The Holy Spirit will come upon you,
and the power of the Most High will overshadow you;
therefore the child to be born will be called holy,
the Son of God.

And behold, your kinswoman Elizabeth in her old age has also conceived a
son; and this is the sixth month with her who was called barren. For with God
nothing will be impossible." And Mary said, "Behold, I am the handmaid of the
Lord; let it be to me according to your word." And the angel departed from her.

Reflection

When the angel appeared to Mary, she did not know what his visit might mean. She probably felt unsure and a little confused. Do you think that once Gabriel explained God's purpose, Mary understood everything in store for her?

Probably not. Yet she said yes to the plan of God, even though she could not understand it completely. Her love and trust were more important than her fear.

Remember Eve? She did not trust God's word. She disobeyed Him when she ate the fruit of the tree in the middle of the garden. She was tempted by the chance to have more knowledge: "You will be like God," Satan promised, "knowing good and evil." (Gen. 3:5)

Mary, on the other hand, trusted, even without full knowledge.

Mary is a model for us of a living faith. When we are unsure or confused, we should turn to her. We ask her to pray for us because she is the mother of God. She is our mother, too. She wants all her children to reach Heaven, and she gives us real help along the way.

Our guardian angels help us, too. God has given each of us a guardian angel who prays for us, protects us from harm, and encourages us to do good things.

Our Lady and the guardian angels are in God's presence all the time. We ask them for help because we know how close they are to our Lord.

Prayer

O Adonai and Ruler of the house of Israel,
You appeared to Moses in the fire of the burning bush,
and on Mount Sinai gave him Your Law.
Come, and with outstretched arm redeem us! Amen. (*O Antiphon for December 18*)

Dig Deeper

Although they are often forgotten, the angels play a pivotal role in salvation history.

A fallen angel, Satan, tempted the first woman to reject God, setting in motion God's plan of rescue. Instrumental to that plan were the angels, who appear over and over in the Old Testament.

Then, when the time of salvation arrived, the angel Gabriel announced the coming of the Messiah (and His forerunner). Angels ministered to Jesus when He was tempted in the desert and were with Him continually.

The work of angels was not over after Christ's Resurrection and Ascension. They continue to minister to us, and Christ tells us that each one of us has a guardian angel (see Matt. 18:10). Our guardian angels protect and guide us throughout our lives. Let us pray to this heavenly companion and ask God to strengthen him in his role for our salvation.

Mary

(Lilies)

Song of Solomon 2:1–2

I am a rose of Sharon,
a lily of the valleys.

As a lily among brambles,
so is my love among maidens.

Reflection

For thousands of years God prepared the world for the coming of His Son. As the time drew near for the birth of our Lord, God created Mary in the womb of her mother. God did not allow her to be stained by Original Sin. It was through the grace of her own Son's work that our Lady received this gift. This unique privilege of Mary is called the Immaculate Conception.

Our Lord is the only person in the history of the world who chose His own mother. As His followers—His sisters and brothers—we are blessed to call her our mother, too.

He gave her to us from the Cross. Speaking to her and to His beloved disciple John, He said, "Woman, behold your son!… Behold your mother" (John 19:26-27). Jesus meant that all of His beloved followers—like you and me—should look to Mary as our mother. And we can know that Mary cares for us as her children.

The lily symbolizes the purity of Mary. Purity means doing the right things for the right reasons. Mary's purity flows from the grace of her Immaculate Conception. Her purity was part of every choice our Lady made throughout her life. Each and every one of our Lady's actions and words had always one motivation: the love of God.

During Advent, we can ask God to purify our hearts. We can ask Him to give us a pure heart like our Lady's, so that all we say and do can be pleasing to Him.

Prayer

O Root of Jesse,
You stand for an ensign of mankind;
before You kings shall keep silence,
and to You all nations shall have recourse.
Come, save us, and do not delay. Amen. *(O Antiphon for December 19)*

Dig Deeper

The feast of the Immaculate Conception falls, by divine coincidence, during Advent. The two feasts of the Immaculate Conception and Christmas are intimately connected: one fulfills the promise of a woman who would have "enmity" with the serpent and the other fulfills the promise of the seed who would crush the head of that serpent (see Gen. 3:15).

It was fitting that the mother of God would be immaculately conceived. She was the first tabernacle for the Lord, sheltering Him for nine months in her immaculate womb. No tabernacle on earth, or even in Heaven, is more glorious than the Blessed Virgin Mary.

As we celebrate the feasts of the Immaculate Conception and Christmas, let us make ourselves worthy tabernacles to receive our Lord into our hearts in Holy Communion.

Mary
(Magnificat)

Luke 1:39–56

In those days Mary arose and went with haste into the hill country, to a city of Judah, and she entered the house of Zechari'ah and greeted Elizabeth. And when Elizabeth heard the greeting of Mary, the babe leaped in her womb; and Elizabeth was filled with the Holy Spirit and she exclaimed with a loud cry, "Blessed are you among women, and blessed is the fruit of your womb! And why is this granted me, that the mother of my Lord should come to me? For behold, when the voice of your greeting came to my ears, the babe in my womb leaped for joy. And blessed is she who believed that there would be a fulfilment of what was spoken to her from the Lord." And Mary said,

> "My soul magnifies the Lord,
> and my spirit rejoices in God my Savior,
> for he has regarded the low estate of his handmaiden.
> For behold, henceforth all generations will call me blessed;
> for he who is mighty has done great things for me,
> and holy is his name.
> And his mercy is on those who fear him
> from generation to generation.
> He has shown strength with his arm,
> he has scattered the proud in the imagination of their hearts,
> he has put down the mighty from their thrones,
> and exalted those of low degree;
> he has filled the hungry with good things,
> and the rich he has sent empty away.
> He has helped his servant Israel,
> in remembrance of his mercy,
> as he spoke to our fathers,
> to Abraham and to his posterity for ever."

And Mary remained with her about three months, and returned to her home.

Reflection

When Mary met her cousin Elizabeth, it was her first chance to tell someone about the great privilege she had received—becoming the mother of the Lord.

Elizabeth had already experienced a miracle of her own. Now, the Holy Spirit, with the assistance of the leaping, unborn John the Baptist, inspired her to see that the blessing was even greater than she first thought. It's not just an elderly couple bearing a child in their old age who will grow up to serve the Lord. Somehow, "the mother of [the] Lord" was standing on her doorstep.

Today's ornament is called Magnificat. We see on it a picture of Mary in prayer. The ornament is named Magnificat because of the prayer of Mary we read in our Scripture passage: "My soul magnifies the Lord, and my spirit rejoices in God my Savior."

The Latin word *magnificat* means "magnifies." To magnify something is to enlarge it. We often think of magnifying as a way to make something easier to see.

Mary truly does magnify the Lord for us. Under the Old Covenant, the Chosen People knew much about God, but there were many things they could not know, because God had not yet sent His Son. Now, because of Mary's yes, for the people of the New Covenant, God will be easier to see. He has become like us in all things but sin. He has taken on flesh—the flesh of Mary His mother.

We can magnify the Lord in our lives, too. By our words and actions, we can make Christ easier for others to see.

Prayer

O Key of David and Scepter of the house of Israel:
You open and no one closes;
You close and no one opens.
Come, and deliver him from the chains of prison who sits in darkness and
in the shadow of death. Amen. *(O Antiphon for December 20)*

Dig Deeper

Mary's Magnificat speaks of the humbling of the mighty and the raising up of the lowly. We find this theme throughout salvation history, most particularly in the Song of Hannah (1 Sam. 2:4–5), which includes the words,

> *The bows of the mighty are broken,*
> *   but the feeble gird on strength.*
> *Those who were full have hired themselves out for bread,*
> *   but those who were hungry have ceased to hunger.*
> *The barren has borne seven,*
> *   but she who has many children is forlorn.*

The upending of the normal order of this world is the way of the Lord. His Chosen People were a small, insignificant tribe. He sent His Son to be born in a manger to an unknown peasant mother. Jesus selected mostly uneducated workmen to be His ambassadors to the world. By all human logic, God's efforts should be failures.

As St. Paul says, "For the foolishness of God is wiser than men, and the weakness of God is stronger than men" (1 Cor. 1:25). It is precisely through human weakness that God's power is revealed. Only when we humble ourselves will we be lifted up, as Hannah and Mary were.

John
the Baptist

(Baptismal Font)

Luke 1:57–80

Now the time came for Elizabeth to be delivered, and she gave birth to a son. And her neighbors and kinsfolk heard that the Lord had shown great mercy to her, and they rejoiced with her. And on the eighth day they came to circumcise the child; and they would have named him Zechari'ah after his father, but his mother said, "Not so; he shall be called John." And they said to her, "None of your kindred is called by this name." And they made signs to his father, inquiring what he would have him called. And he asked for a writing tablet, and wrote, "His name is John." And they all marveled. And immediately his mouth was opened and his tongue loosed, and he spoke, blessing God. And fear came on all their neighbors. And all these things were talked about through all the hill country of Judea; and all who heard them laid them up in their hearts, saying, "What then will this child be?" For the hand of the Lord was with him.

And his father Zechari'ah was filled with the Holy Spirit, and prophesied, saying,

*"Blessed be the Lord God of Israel,
for he has visited and redeemed his people,
and has raised up a horn of salvation for us
in the house of his servant David,
as he spoke by the mouth of his holy prophets from of old,
that we should be saved from our enemies,
and from the hand of all who hate us;
to perform the mercy promised to our fathers,
and to remember his holy covenant,
the oath which he swore to our father Abraham, to grant us
that we, being delivered from the hand of our enemies,
might serve him without fear,
in holiness and righteousness before him all the days of our life.*

And you, child, will be called the prophet of the Most High;
for you will go before the Lord to prepare his ways,
to give knowledge of salvation to his people
in the forgiveness of their sins,
through the tender mercy of our God,
when the day shall dawn upon us from on high
to give light to those who sit in darkness and in the shadow of death,
to guide our feet into the way of peace."

And the child grew and became strong in spirit, and he was in
the wilderness till the day of his manifestation to Israel.

Reflection

In today's Scripture we read the joyful prayer of Zechariah: his first spoken words after the birth of John the Baptist. The first part of this prayer is about God; the second part is about John himself. And both parts are also about God's people.

Zechariah first tells of the goodness of God and God's long-spoken desire to save His people. The Savior was coming, from among His own kingly people. And it was happening just as He had always promised, going all the way back to Abraham.

At last, the time had come when God's people could know both holiness and righteousness. These things are impossible to have without God's life in the soul. Christ will make possible this life.

Then Zechariah's prayer speaks of John. Inspired by the Holy Spirit, he says that his son will be a prophet of the coming Messiah, preparing His way. He will let people know that salvation is possible, that it is coming soon. He will preach the forgiveness of sins, because now forgiveness is to be available to all men, in all places, in all times.

The Chosen People lived for a long time in darkness and turmoil, but now light is dawning, "peace among men with whom he is pleased" (Luke 2:14).

Prayer

O Rising Dawn, Radiance of the Light eternal and Sun of Justice;
come, and enlighten those who sit in darkness and in the shadow of death.
   Amen. (*O Antiphon for December 21*)

Dig Deeper

Our Lord said that "among those born of women there has risen no one greater than John the Baptist" (Matt. 11:11). This is because his mission was the greatest task ever given to man: to be the forerunner of Christ, to announce His coming to the world.

John the Baptist lived a life of extreme asceticism in order to be strong enough for the task given to him. During Advent we too have been called to asceticism as we prepare for the coming of Christ at Christmas. We seek to break our attachment to the physical world in order to be more united to Christ.

Christ also said of John the Baptist, "yet he who is least in the kingdom of heaven is greater than he" (Matt. 11:11). As great as John the Baptist was, he did not live under the New Covenant, when the graces of the sacraments would be available to all of Christ's followers. This supernatural grace builds on the foundation of our self-denial, allowing us to unite to Christ in a way impossible even for John the Baptist.

Joseph

(Carpenter's Tools)

Matthew 1:18–25

*Now the birth of Jesus Christ took place in this way. When his mother Mary
had been betrothed to Joseph, before they came together she was found to
be with child of the Holy Spirit; and her husband Joseph, being a just man
and unwilling to put her to shame, resolved to send her away quietly. But
as he considered this, behold, an angel of the Lord appeared to him in a
dream, saying, "Joseph, son of David, do not fear to take Mary your wife,
for that which is conceived in her is of the Holy Spirit; she will bear a son,
and you shall call his name Jesus, for he will save his people from their sins."
All this took place to fulfil what the Lord had spoken by the prophet:*

*"Behold, a virgin shall conceive and bear a son,
and his name shall be called Emman'u-el"*

*(which means, God with us). When Joseph woke from sleep, he did
as the angel of the Lord commanded him; he took his wife, but knew
her not until she had borne a son; and he called his name Jesus.*

Reflection

Every father is the protector of his family. He shields his wife and children from dangers to body and soul. He provides for their physical needs and also for their spiritual needs, leading them in the ways of God.

Imagine Joseph realizing that he was to be protector of the Holy Family: a wife who was sinless and all-pure, and a Son who was conceived by the power "of the Holy Spirit." Was he nervous to take on such a serious responsibility?

We know that up to this moment in his life he had been "a just man"—he always wanted to live in a way pleasing to God. So, when he awoke from the dream, it was not strange for him to do "as the angel of the Lord commanded him." This was how he had always lived. So it was also how he stepped into his new vocation as husband of our Lady and earthly father of our Lord.

Sometimes Joseph seems to be forgotten, even by followers of Christ. He did not make astounding prophecies. He didn't heal people or preach amazing sermons. Those things were not what God asked of him.

But what God did ask, and what Joseph did, turned out to be more glorious than the mission of any saint after our Lady. He sheltered Mary, who bore the Son of God. And he raised Jesus, the boy who would be "the Son of Man."

Prayer

O King of the Gentiles and the Desired of all,
You are the cornerstone that binds two into one.
Come, and save poor Man whom You fashioned out of clay. Amen.
(*O Antiphon for December 22*)

Dig Deeper

St. Joseph was one of the greatest saints who ever lived. He has been an example of manhood, action, and faithfulness for all generations. Yet Scripture records not one word he ever spoke. He is the "silent saint."

This is a lesson for us all. It is not our words that are our primary witness to sanctity, but our actions. St. Josemaría Escrivá said, "Love means deeds, not sweet words." St. Joseph backed his love for the Blessed Mother and our Lord with his deeds: protecting and providing for them, and leading them as the head of the Holy Family.

Let us put our faith into action, professing our love for the Lord not just with our words, but with our deeds.

The Wise Men

(Star of Bethlehem)

Matthew 2:1–12

Now when Jesus was born in Bethlehem of Judea in the days of Herod the king, behold, wise men from the East came to Jerusalem, saying, "Where is he who has been born king of the Jews? For we have seen his star in the East, and have come to worship him." When Herod the king heard this, he was troubled, and all Jerusalem with him; and assembling all the chief priests and scribes of the people, he inquired of them where the Christ was to be born. They told him, "In Bethlehem of Judea; for so it is written by the prophet:

'And you, O Bethlehem, in the land of Judah,
are by no means least among the rulers of Judah;
for from you shall come a ruler
who will govern my people Israel.'"

Then Herod summoned the wise men secretly and ascertained from them what time the star appeared; and he sent them to Bethlehem, saying, "Go and search diligently for the child, and when you have found him bring me word, that I too may come and worship him." When they had heard the king they went their way; and lo, the star which they had seen in the East went before them, till it came to rest over the place where the child was. When they saw the star, they rejoiced exceedingly with great joy; and going into the house they saw the child with Mary his mother, and they fell down and worshiped him. Then, opening their treasures, they offered him gifts, gold and frankincense and myrrh. And being warned in a dream not to return to Herod, they departed to their own country by another way.

Reflection

Jesus was the promised Son of David, the Messiah of the Chosen People of Israel. But His mission was not only to save the Chosen People. His mission would be even greater. It reached far beyond Israel to the ends of the earth, as God had promised Abraham long ago.

The Star of Bethlehem symbolized the great reach of God's work of salvation: it stretched to the very heavens and was proclaimed to people in faraway lands. The three wise men who came to adore Jesus showed that all nations of the earth will give glory to God.

Today's Scripture tells us of three gifts the wise men brought to the newborn king. What were they?

Gold, frankincense, and myrrh were each extremely valuable. In fact the myrrh, not the gold, was probably the most expensive of the three.

Gold is proper to a king; incense is for worship; and myrrh is for the burial of the dead. In the three gifts we see the unique identity of the Messiah: He is King, God, and Sacrifice.

We too can give these gifts to our Lord. We can give Him gold when we ask Him to rule in our hearts, making Him king of our lives. We give Him frankincense when we worship Him with pure hearts. We offer Him myrrh when we love our crucified Lord and adore Him at the Holy Sacrifice of the Mass.

Prayer

O Emmanuel, our King and Lawgiver,
the Expected of nations and their Savior:
Come, and save us, O Lord our God! Amen.
(O Antiphon for December 23)

Dig Deeper

On January 6 we celebrate the feast of the Epiphany. The *Catechism of the Catholic Church* says of this feast:

> *The great feast of Epiphany celebrates the adoration of Jesus by the wise men* (magi) *from the East, together with his baptism in the Jordan and the wedding feast at Cana in Galilee.* (CCC 528)

These three events are intrinsically linked—each is the manifestation (or epiphany) of Jesus as the Savior of the world. The Magi were gentile rulers who recognized the true King of Kings. At the Baptism of the Lord, all those present witnessed the divine "endorsement," so to speak, of Christ by the Father. And at the wedding at Cana, Jesus manifested His divine, miraculous powers in public for the first time.

As we remember the coming of the Magi, let us see in it the manifestation of God's saving work to the whole world.

Let us put our faith into action, professing our love for the Lord not just with our words, but with our deeds.

Baby Jesus

(Manger)

Luke 2:1–19

In those days a decree went out from Caesar Augustus that all the world should be enrolled. This was the first enrollment, when Quirin'i-us was governor of Syria. And all went to be enrolled, each to his own city. And Joseph also went up from Galilee, from the city of Nazareth, to Judea, to the city of David, which is called Bethlehem, because he was of the house and lineage of David, to be enrolled with Mary, his betrothed, who was with child. And while they were there, the time came for her to be delivered. And she gave birth to her first-born son and wrapped him in swaddling cloths, and laid him in a manger, because there was no place for them in the inn.

And in that region there were shepherds out in the field, keeping watch over their flock by night. And an angel of the Lord appeared to them, and the glory of the Lord shone around them, and they were filled with fear. And the angel said to them, "Be not afraid; for behold, I bring you good news of a great joy which will come to all the people; for to you is born this day in the city of David a Savior, who is Christ the Lord. And this will be a sign for you: you will find a babe wrapped in swaddling cloths and lying in a manger." And suddenly there was with the angel a multitude of the heavenly host praising God and saying,

"Glory to God in the highest,
and on earth peace among men with whom he is pleased!"

When the angels went away from them into heaven, the shepherds said to one another, "Let us go over to Bethlehem and see this thing that has happened, which the Lord has made known to us." And they went with haste, and found Mary and Joseph, and the babe lying in a manger. And when they saw it they made known the saying which had been told them concerning this child; and all who heard it wondered at what the shepherds told them. But Mary kept all these things, pondering them in her heart.

Reflection

When the first son of an earthly king is born, the whole kingdom celebrates. Yet the Son of the Eternal King, who would become the King of Kings and Lord of Lords, is born in a lonely stable.

Why a stable?

Because in the crowded town of Bethlehem, no one offered Joseph and Mary a place to stay. There was no room for them in an inn, and not a single person gave them a place indoors. Can you think of some reasons why?

Maybe they were busy with other visitors. Maybe it seemed scary or strange to take in a woman who was about to give birth.

The people of Bethlehem had understandable reasons for failing to welcome the Holy Family. How could they really know who it was they were refusing?

We don't have these excuses, yet sometimes we can fail to welcome Jesus, Mary, and Joseph, too. When we sin, we close the door of our hearts to the Holy Family. But through the grace of Christ's life and death, we can always have another chance. We can always choose again to open the door to our Lord.

Though few people on earth rejoiced at Christ's birth, in Heaven the angels rejoiced. They knew that at last salvation had come to the world. The fulfillment of all the Old Testament promises is now here—the Root of Jesse is born! Let us rejoice with the angels! Open wide the doors to Christ!

Prayer

O Lord,
You make us happy every year in the expectation of our redemption.
We welcome joyfully as our Redeemer your only-begotten Son, our Lord Jesus Christ.
Give us the grace to be without fear when we see Him coming again to judge us. Amen. (*Collect, Vigil of Christmas*)

Dig Deeper

After St. Joseph discovered the pregnancy of Mary, an angel came to him, told him to take Mary as his wife, and said, "you shall call his name Jesus, for he will save his people from their sins" (Matt. 1:21).

The name *Jesus* means "the Lord saves" or just "savior," and it is the most perfect name for this baby born in Bethlehem. Ever since the Fall of Adam and Eve, the world had been in desperate need of salvation. We have no power to save ourselves—we are helpless in the face of sin and death.

In His mercy, though, God sent His own Son to be our Savior, to lift us up to Him. As St. Athanasius said, "For the Son of God became man so that we might become God."

Sophia Institute

Sophia Institute is a nonprofit institution that seeks to nurture the spiritual, moral, and cultural life of souls and to spread the Gospel of Christ in conformity with the authentic teachings of the Roman Catholic Church.

Sophia Institute Press fulfills this mission by offering translations, reprints, and new publications that afford readers a rich source of the enduring wisdom of mankind.

Sophia Institute also operates the popular online resource CatholicExchange.com. *Catholic Exchange* provides world news from a Catholic perspective as well as daily devotionals and articles that will help readers to grow in holiness and live a life consistent with the teachings of the Church.

In 2013, Sophia Institute launched Sophia Institute for Teachers to renew and rebuild Catholic culture through service to Catholic education. With the goal of nurturing the spiritual, moral, and cultural life of souls, and an abiding respect for the role and work of teachers, we strive to provide materials and programs that are at once enlightening to the mind and ennobling to the heart; faithful and complete, as well as useful and practical.

Sophia Institute gratefully recognizes the Solidarity Association for preserving and encouraging the growth of our apostolate over the course of many years. Without their generous and timely support, this book would not be in your hands.

www.SophiaInstitute.com
www.CatholicExchange.com
www.SophiaInstituteforTeachers.org

Sophia Institute Press® is a registered trademark of Sophia Institute. Sophia Institute is a tax-exempt institution as defined by the Internal Revenue Code, Section 501(c)(3). Tax ID 22-2548708.

Please see the following pages for Jesse Tree ornaments and images that you can cut out and display in your home to further assist you in your Advent devotions.

Adam and Eve
Apple

Gabriel
Angel

Aaron
Hand of Blessing

**John
the Baptist**
Baptismal Font

Nehemiah
Church

Zechariah
Censer

Solomon
Crown

Joseph
Coat of Many Colors

David
Harp

Messiah
Dawn

Joseph
Carpenter's Tools

Ezekiel
Heart of Flesh

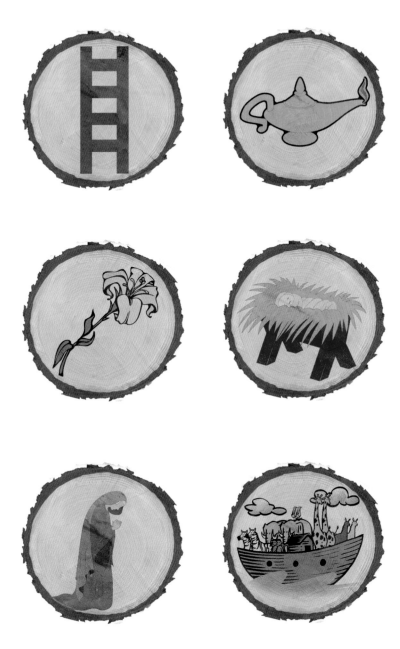

Samuel
Lamp

Jacob
Ladder

Baby Jesus
Manger

Mary
Lilies

Noah
Ark

Mary
Magnificat

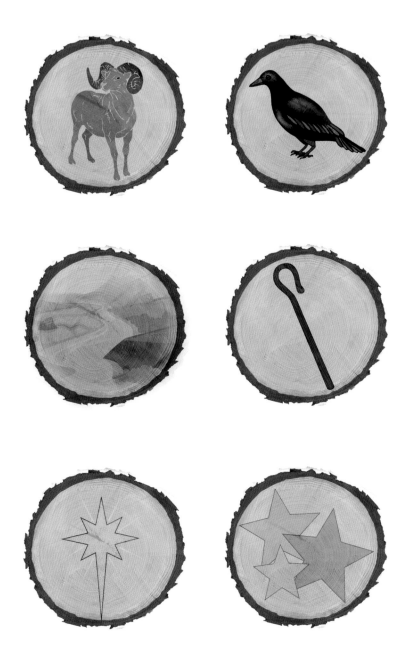

Elijah
Raven

Isaac
Ram

**The
Good Shepherd**
Staff

**New
Covenant**
River

Abraham
Stars

**The
Wise Men**
Star of Bethlehem

Isaiah
Tongs

Moses
Tablets

Creation
World

Absolon Stumme, Tree of Jesse, Hamburg Cathedral Polyptych, ca.1499. Musée de Varsovie, tempura and gold leaf on panel, public domain.

Flemish Breviary, ca. 1500, Bibliothèque Royale (Pays-Bas), illuminated manuscript, public domain.

l'arbre de Jessé, ca. 1180, Bible des capucins, illuminated manuscript, public domain.